WHY BE GOOD, WHEN EVERYONE ELSE GOES
ALONG WITH THE CROWD?

AREN'T DIVORCE, DRINKING AND PRE-
MARITAL SEX JUST FACTS OF LIFE TODAY?

DON'T STATUS AND SUCCESS MAKE
EVERYDAY HONESTY OUT-OF-DATE?

In *Sin, Sex and Self-Control*, America's "Minister to Millions" tackles the human questions
that grow directly out of the new freedoms of the
1960s. "Inevitably this is a bestseller," writes
Dr. Daniel Poling, "but more importantly it
may become the moral pivot of our time." *Sin,
Sex and Self-Control* is an inspired guide to confident living *today*—a personal challenge that
can help you change your own destiny.

NORMAN VINCENT PEALE

SIN, SEX AND SELF-CONTROL

FAWCETT CREST • NEW YORK

SIN, SEX AND SELF-CONTROL

Published by Fawcett Crest Books, a unit of CBS Publications,
the Consumer Publishing Division of CBS, Inc.,
by arrangement with Doubleday & Company

This book contains the complete text of the original hardcover edition.

ISBN: 0-449-23921-7

Printed in the United States of America

20   19   18   17   16   15   14   13

This book is more than the work of one man. It is rather the joint endeavor of a dedicated and harmonious "team," one that has planned, thought, researched, and worked together for many months. I owe an enormous debt of gratitude to my cherished friends: Arthur Gordon, highly skilled and notable writer, and John M. Allen, keen and sensitive Associate Editor of the *Reader's Digest;* and to my beloved wife, Ruth Stafford Peale, perceptive and always challenging in her insights.

To work with these three on the vital subject treated in this book has been one of the most meaningful experiences of my life.

Norman Vincent Peale

CONTENTS

SIN,
SEX AND
SELF-CONTROL

CHAPTER I

The Moral Crisis around Us

Not long ago I came to a period of profound concern and uneasiness in my life. Everywhere I went, it seemed, people were asking me what was wrong with America—indeed, what was wrong with the world. Divorce statistics, crime statistics, the erosion of honesty, race relations, the collapse of sex morals—these and a thousand other proofs of modern man's inability to cope with himself or his environment were constantly being brought to my attention with earnest and anxious pleas for an explanation or a solution. And I knew—when I was really honest with myself—that I was not supplying the answers.

For more than forty years, ever since my ordination, I had been preaching that if a person would surrender to Jesus Christ and adopt strong affirmative attitudes toward life he would be able to live abundantly and triumphantly. I was still absolutely convinced that this was true. But I was also bleakly aware that the whole trend of this seventh decade of the twentieth century seemed to be away from the principles and practices of religion—not toward them.

Whenever I am depressed or discouraged, something in me instinctively turns to the land. Perhaps it's because I was born in a little country town in Ohio and spent my formative years close to the dark, rich soil that covers the heartland of America. Anyway, I have never been able to live without some contact with it. Almost thirty years ago, soon after I was called to the Marble Collegiate Church in New York, I borrowed some money and acquired an old farmhouse in Dutchess County, seventy-five miles from the city. Towering maples lean over that house, deep green in summer, flame-colored in autumn. From the front porch I can look out across the rolling foothills of the Berkshires. A great barn across the road cuts off part of the view, but that is as it should be. After all, a barn is an act of faith, a symbol of man's trust in the goodness and bounty of God.

So, when I am troubled, I try to leave the teeming city with its noise and confusion and go back to Sugar Tree Farm. And even if the troubles do not go away, something in my soul almost always finds the strength and the serenity to endure them.

This time, I came alone. My wife was in Texas, making a speech. Two of our children are married, now; the third was finishing her last year at college. I came in the long spring twilight; the evening was calm and still; the scent of lilac was in the air.

For a while I sat at my desk, trying to outline next Sunday's sermon. In my pocket was a fragment that I had torn that morning from a metropolitan newspaper. It was an advertisement—a big, bold one—for a book that has been known for decades as one of literature's most lurid examples of pornography. The advertisement stated triumphantly that the New York courts had ruled that the book could be sold without hindrance. It was in my mind to speak out against this decision and express the contempt I felt for the publisher from the pulpit of my church.

But the ideas did not come easily, or arrange themselves as they should. Too much was weighing on my mind. Finally I left my desk and went out on the front porch. Beyond the great barn a full moon was rising, soft on the gentle hills. The scene was tranquil and familiar and full of peace, but I found myself remembering the man who had come up to me after my last speaking engagement in a Midwestern town. "Doctor," he had said abruptly, "do you think we've had it?" I asked him what he meant, although I was fairly sure that I knew. "Look around you," he said, amost angrily. "Can't you read the signs? We're rich and powerful and prosperous, sure. But so was Babylon. So was Rome. Where will this country be a hundred years from now? Or even fifty? You know what I think? I think God is fed up with us!" I could still see that man's face, still hear his voice.

I walked down the flagstone path and stood by the white fence with my hand on the gate. Was God really turning His face away from us? I couldn't believe it. Along with infinite love, surely, went infinite hope, infinite compassion, infinite patience. No, if anything, in all the confusion, all the apparent decay, God was trying to tell us something, show us something. I was sure of it.

But what?

The shadows were darker, now; the tree frogs were croaking and chirping. A rabbit hopped out into the road, saw me, and ducked back into the bushes. The moon rode high, its arid plains and mountain ranges clearly visible. For billions of years it had been circling the earth, never varying, always turning the same face. Even its eclipses were orderly, predictable. The great clock of the universe was never fast, never slow. All around me I felt the marvelous balance and rhythm of nature, but this only served to deepen my discouragement. Why and how, with so much harmony all around him, did man contrive to make such a mess of things?

I stood there at the gate for a long time. On either hand the road stretched away, silver in the moonlight. Finally I began to walk along it, my footsteps loud in the quiet night. Here and there, through the trees, a light shone from a neighbor's house. In those houses were people, human beings like myself, worried sometimes, puzzled often, groping for answers. There was nothing fully predictable about the life of any one of them, none of the order or certainty that governed the rest of nature. And for one reason only. The moon obeyed the laws of gravity. The rabbit in the road was controlled by instinct; so was the owl that might swoop upon the rabbit. But man had been given freedom of choice. He alone could alter his environment or change his future, because God had given him a will of his own—and left it free.

I came to a place where the road forked, and stopped. Here I was, a sovereign human being. I could choose to go left. Or I could choose to go right. No authority was there to compel me. No law of gravity tugged me one way or the other. I was free to choose.

This freedom . . . something seemed to glimmer in my mind. Wasn't it possible that much of the moral confusion of our times was the result of too much freedom, achieved too suddenly? Wasn't it possible that in rebelling against the old authoritarianisms of the past, man had neglected his own inner controls? Wouldn't that explain these signs of apparent degeneration, these stupid, harmful, selfish acts that distressed all thinking, God-fearing people?

It might be true. But even if it were, might not this trend also be a hopeful thing, a sign that man was groping his way toward a new maturity? In the past, people had been kept from unwise action through commands, threats, punishments, subjugation, ostracism—even burning at the stake. Was it possible that we were reaching out toward a new era of self-imposed restraints—and suffering sharp growing pains in the process?

This dim concept of our society moving ahead, rather than back, sent a flicker of excitement through me. And gradually, standing there in the moonlight, I began to see it more clearly. The times weren't *really* out of joint; this new freedom wasn't *really* at fault. It was how we handled it that mattered, whether we used or abused it, whether we grew with it in strength and confidence or regressed to uncontrolled, unthinking, uncaring selfishness.

My fingers touched the fragment of newsprint in my pocket. My reaction to the advertisement of that pornographic book had been direct and simple and valid. No parent in his right mind would want that book in his home where impressionable children might read it. But maybe it was the parent's job to make that decision. Maybe the parent should have freedom to say no. In the last analysis, that was what the court had done. It had shifted responsibility from the law to the individual. It did not say that the book was a good thing. It simply removed a restraint. It was acting on the assumption that the individual would be able to make the right choice.

Was that assumption valid? I stood there, groping for an answer. It might be valid if . . . if people were civilized and disciplined enough. If people could realize that when such restraints were removed they would have to restrain themselves. If they could be shown how to do this, and helped to do it, and made to see what an exciting thing this new way of life could be. Not imposed restrictions. Self-control.

Again I felt a little prickle of excitement go shivering down my spine. What a challenge, and what an opportunity! It was almost as if God were saying to man, "All right, here is a new test, a new trial, a new choice. Here you are on the threshold of a magnificent new maturity. You can step across it—or not. You can go down, like the Babylonians, like the Romans—or forward, with your strength and self-mastery increasing with each new test. Which shall it be?"

And was the question so very new? Two thousand years ago a Man went up and down the dusty roads of Judea and Galilee telling people how to live. He laid no harsh prohibitions on them. He did not castigate them for their mistakes. He merely told them to live—to love God, love one another, love themselves. One day, on the side of a mountain, He preached a sermon in which He outlined certain disciplines that would enable a person to follow this rule of love. Even then, He spoke gently. He uttered no threats. "Happy is he who does this," He said; "blessed is he who does that." And it was this same Man who said, "The kingdom of heaven is within you."

I turned back toward the lights of Sugar Tree Farm with a hundred splintered thoughts whirling in my mind. The collapse of external restraints combined with the absence of internal disciplines—could not this explain most of the problems of our time? From race riots to divorces to income tax cheating, was there any area of modern life where this interpretation failed to fit? And if it did fit, might not a book be written that would take up the major areas of modern life—marriage, family relations, personal honesty, sex attitudes—examine the erosion there, and suggest what a person might do to reverse the trend by strengthening and disciplining himself?

It was out of the thoughts and emotions of that soft spring night that the decision to write this book was born. Much of what I shall have to say in the following pages may sound somber and discouraging, but I write with a feeling of enormous hope and confidence. Implicit in the confusion that surrounds us, shining through all the disintegration and decay, is a marvelous opportunity—to bend the curve of destiny back up!

It will never be easy; it will require courage and sacrifice and struggle. But from that struggle, to those who undertake it, will come an enormous surge of strength and self-confidence. For God, in His infinite wisdom, has created man so that he lives most abundantly, most satisfyingly, when he *is* faced with choices, when he *is* under pressure, when he *is* meeting a challenge.

"He who rules his spirit," says the Bible, "is better than he who takes a city." Along this path of individual self-mastery, I truly believe, lies the destiny and salvation of our modern world.

MEMO TO THE READER NO. 1

"The Biggest Dividend in the World"

You know, whenever I try to write a book or prepare a sermon I like to visualize my audience—you. I like to think of you as a friend, sitting with me, listening to me, talking back to me once in a while. That way I feel closer to you, and I hope you feel closer to me.

So in this book I'm going to try an experiment—an experiment in closeness! Now and then, instead of writing a whole chapter, I'm going to write informal notes to you. Just talk off the cuff, say whatever comes into my head about almost anything. Maybe we'll get to know each other better that way. And maybe it will help us understand the theme of the book more personally, more deeply.

From the start, I knew that this was going to be a demanding book. It wasn't merely going to say things that the reader could agree with, nod his head sagely, and turn the page unchanged. It was going to ask him to survey himself—with discontent. It was going to call on him to do something about his personality and character and the innermost fiber of his being—that is to say, his soul.

Would people be willing to respond to such a challenge? Would they even want to try? These questions troubled me so much that one night, when a few friends came to dinner, I outlined the theme of the book: my conviction that the apparent decline of morality stemmed from a widespread rejection of the old rules and authorities, and that the only way out of our difficulties was to move forward to a new enlightenment in which people would learn to govern themselves.

The initial reactions that I got were encouraging, but I did not take these too seriously: people are kind-hearted; besides, I was the host and they were eating my food! No, it was the *delayed* reactions that I found exciting.

For example, a couple of weeks after that evening, I met

16

one of our women guests again. "You know," she said, "that self-discipline idea that we were talking about . . . it's been on my mind. I find myself wondering all the time if what I'm doing in a given situation is what a controlled person would do. Take the matter of dieting, for instance. I've always been a half-hearted dieter—take off a few pounds, then give up and gain them right back. Guess I was like the heavy woman who said she had taken off forty pounds: that is, five pounds off, eight times. But thinking about this in the light of our discussion, I began to see that in the past I was always vaguely looking for some external authority that would *compel* me to lose weight. You helped me to realize that there actually isn't any such authority—except me! It's a wonderful thought—sort of freeing, if you know what I mean. So I said to myself, 'Who's going to be boss around here, your appetite or you?' For the first time in my life, I found myself controlling my eating; I've lost six pounds, and I know I'm not going to gain them back. I've won a victory, and I'm proud of myself, and I feel great!"

"You look great, too," I said. And she did.

Then a day or two later one of the men said to me, "This idea of applying discipline to yourself . . . by George, once you start thinking about it it creeps in everywhere! The other day I was driving along a road where the speed limit is sixty miles per hour. No other cars were in sight. No cops, either. So I began to push down on the accelerator, and the speedometer needle crept up to seventy. But then I said to myself, 'Wait a minute, now. You're not in control. You're breaking the law. You're endangering your own life and maybe others. You're being pretty stupid and selfish, aren't you? Does it take a motorcycle cop behind you to make you act like a civilized human being? So I slowed down to sixty. And from now on, that's the way I'm going to drive."

And a third guest said, "This question of self-responsibility . . . I'd never thought too much about it before. But yesterday, through some oversight, the conductor on my train didn't pick up my ticket. Now, a month ago I'd have said to myself, 'Good; a free ride.' And I'd have put my ticket in my pocket. But yesterday I got up and went looking for the conductor and gave him my ticket. Why? Because I decided I wanted to jack my standards up just that one little notch. And the amazing thing is, it hurts for a minute when you first try it, but then you feel a glow that more than makes up for it. You invest a little will power, and you get back the biggest dividend in the world!"

It hurts for a minute, the man said. Sure it does, if it's a small change of attitude. A big change hurts longer than that. You have to pay the price of self-improvement, which is pain, before you can claim the reward, which is power. But each of these three people had tried a small experiment in self-discipline—and in each case it worked wonders.

It can work wonders for you, too, if you will try it soberly and sincerely. The experiment will never be finished; each time you reach a rung above the one you've been standing on, there will be a rung above that. But my friend was right: a sense of self-mastery *is* the greatest dividend in the world. It's worth any effort, any sacrifice. "Self-reverence," wrote Tennyson, "self-knowledge, self-control, these three alone lead life to sovereign power." Of the three, I think the last is the most difficult and the most rewarding.

So if you go forward into this book with me, don't look for magic formulas or easy answers. You won't find them here! What you will find, I believe, is a challenge so exciting and rewarding that it may change your thinking and your attitudes and your whole outlook on the great adventure of life.

So, in the remainder of this book, let's explore the major areas of living that all of us share—marriage, family, children, love, health, sex, and the rest—and see if we can't apply some of Tennyson's wisdom to them. And let's start with one of the most fundamental areas of all: personal honesty in daily life.

CHAPTER II

The Twilight of Honesty

A few weeks ago, I came upon my son John shaking his head over something he was reading in the newspaper. "Listen to this," he said. "It says here that every year in this country thieving workers steal at least a billion dollars in cash or merchandise from their employers. Every single *day*, white-collar workers get away with about four million dollars. One insurance company estimates that over a thousand businesses failed last year because of losses caused by dishonest employees. What do you think of that?"

"Not much," I admitted.

John folded the newspaper moodily. "Do you know what I think? I think dishonesty is a contagious disease. And we're living in the middle of an epidemic!"

"Does the newspaper suggest a cure?"

John frowned. "The editorial talks about tougher judges, longer jail sentences, that sort of thing. But it seems to me that those deterrents don't really work. Somehow we have to get inside people's heads and make them see how selfish and stupid and ultimately self-defeating dishonesty really is."

"Or conversely," I said, "how challenging and exciting and energizing true honesty can be."

"Right. But it's an enormous job. Discouraging, really."

"Listen," I said to him. "What would you say if I suggested that there are hopeful aspects to this epidemic of dishonesty?"

He raised a skeptical eyebrow. "Oh, come now, Dad. That's carrying positive thinking pretty far!"

"Maybe," I said. "But let me ask you a few questions. You believe in evolution, don't you? You believe that God, Who must have His reasons, has brought life on this planet all the way up from the amoeba to the troubled, confused, complicated, searching creature called man—right?"

"Why, yes," said John, "I believe that."

19

"But evolution isn't always a smooth, upward progression, necessarily. It goes through periods where there is no progress, where in fact it seems to go backward—correct?"

"Sure," said John, "I'll buy that."

"Well," I said, "what if this decline of morals all around us is one of those periods of apparent retreat, a painful but necessary transition between a fairly orderly past, in which people were controlled mainly by external rules and authority, and a far more civilized and enlightened future in which people will finally learn to control themselves?"

"It's an interesting idea," John said cautiously. "Pretty optimistic, though."

"Not unreasonably so," I said. "If you concede that the great over-all trend of evolution is always upward from the primitive to the more complex, then I think that maybe this theory makes a lot of sense. We're in a period of transition, a violent and turbulent one. There has been a drastic rebellion against all authority and all restraints. Maybe those restraints were too rigid, maybe the need for them was never properly explained. But now they're breaking down. And as they drop away, there's bound to be a time lag in which a great many people misuse their new privileges and abuse their new freedom. The birth pangs of any new order are often prolonged and severe—look at the French Revolution, for example. But God has a way of bringing good things out of bad. Maybe that's what He's doing now."

"Do you actually think people have what it takes to control themselves?" John asked slowly. "You're putting a tremendous amount of confidence in the individual, aren't you?"

"Yes," I admitted. "But so does Christianity. When Jesus walked this earth two thousand years ago, He lived in one of the most rule-ridden societies the world has ever seen. But He didn't seem to be concerned with all those external controls. Sometimes He simply brushed them aside."

John smiled. "The Sabbath was made for man, not man for the Sabbath."

"Exactly. It was the internal controls that Jesus talked about. His whole message was summed up in two great commandments: love God and love your fellow man. Now, nobody can compel you to do this. No external authority can make you. But if everyone chose to do it—and really did it—the need for all the other rules would drop away."

"I agree," said John thoughtfully. "But I'm afraid we have a long, long way to go."

That's true, of course; we do have a long way to go. At the moment we are living in a twilight world where the old black-and-white, right-or-wrong patterns of behavior seem to have merged into an ugly and menacing gray. I also hope and believe that we are living *through* it. But it's easy to see why thoughtful people become discouraged.

Every year, with a regularity that should be frightening but ends by being monotonous, the statistics released by the Federal Bureau of Investigation show a higher crime rate, especially among young people. These figures can't be brushed aside with the easy observation that there have always been dishonest people in this imperfect world. They indicate that the *percentage* of dishonest people is much higher than it was ten or twenty or thirty years ago.

Sometimes it's the little, trivial, unexpected thing that dramatizes the situation for you. For example, about a year ago I went into a bakery shop in New York and ordered some doughnuts. The saleslady put them in a paper bag and placed the bag on the counter. I tried to pick it up with one hand, fumbling for some change with the other—and discovered that the saleslady was holding the bag with a death-grip which she maintained until I actually brought out the money and handed it to her. Then, and only then, did she release the doughnuts!

I was flabbergasted, and tempted to tell her to keep her darn doughnuts. "Did you really think I might run away with them?" I asked her.

"I'm not paid to think," she said wearily. "I'm paid to do what I'm told. And I'm told not to let go of anything until it's paid for!"

Well, I could feel my Ohio ancestors spinning in their graves, especially my grandfather, Samuel Peale, who ran a general store in Lynchburg, Ohio, and believed in extending credit to everyone on the theory—not always valid even then, I'm afraid—that everyone was just as honest as he was.

But that saleslady's distrust of the public was based on painful reality. A friend of mine who owns a department store in San Diego told me the other day that his losses this year from customer thefts will amount to over $200,000 —a 10 percent rise over the previous year. I heard of another store manager who, in an effort to demonstrate to his clerks the need for constant vigilance, placed a small empty package, attractively wrapped, on a counter. It was promptly stolen. Forty times that day he wrapped similar packages, and forty times each one was stolen!

Now to me the significant thing in the case of shop-lifting is that the external restraints have not been diminished. If anything, they have been doubled or trebled. More detectives. More two-way mirrors. More electronic devices to catch these amateur thieves. Yet the losses continue to mount, even in these times of great prosperity. And why? Because the *inner* restraints have been weakened, in many people, to the point where they have no respect for other people's property; where the criterion is no longer what is wrong or right, but what you can get away with.

Just the other day I heard a little girl about twelve years old describe an episode in which a boat and an out-board motor had been lost in a storm. The man who owned the boat was insured. The child's father, who owned the outboard motor, was not. "But it turned out all right," she said happily. "Daddy signed a bill of sale, pretending he had sold the engine to his friend before the storm. So the friend collected insurance for the boat *and* the motor, and gave some of it to Daddy." The stunning thing to me was that the child apparently saw nothing immoral with this. Why should she? In her eyes, her father could do no wrong.

Or consider what's happening in another field altogether: scholarship aid. Recently a friend of mine who is on the scholarship committee of a well-known university told me three grim little stories of abuses that must be very widespread indeed. In the first, a boy applied to the university authorities for financial help. When they checked with his family to determine the state of their finances, the astonished parents said that they were well able to afford to pay their son's expenses. Whereupon the boy flew into a rage with his parents. His roommate, he said, was receiving aid; he didn't see why he shouldn't too.

In the second case, a girl who had been receiving a $1500-a-year scholarship for four years was about to be graduated. Her supposedly needy family blithely flew from Hawaii, where they lived, to Los Angeles for the happy occasion.

In the third case, word reached the scholarship committee that the father of a boy applying for aid owned a hotel and other properties in Florida worth half a million dollars. So the request was denied. The next year the family applied again, this time submitting a financial statement that showed the hotel operation $50,000 in the red. My friend's dry comment was: "They learned awfully fast!"

But thank God we have other fathers, many of them, I fondly believe, who are made of sterner stuff, who come out of the great old American tradition of ruggedly honest men, the kind that made this country great. In fact I met one on a Fifth Avenue bus the other day. Headed uptown, the bus on which I was riding stopped in front of a big store and promptly filled up. A father and son, a boy about fourteen years old, sat behind me. Excitedly the boy said, "Gosh, Dad, what do you know, I got into the crowd getting on the bus and slipped by the driver. He didn't see me so I still have my fifteen cents."

"Well," said the father, "so my son is just a downright thief, a crook, eh?"

"Oh, Dad, it isn't anything. The bus company is rich; they don't need the money."

"Is that so?" replied the father. "The bus company has only one thing to sell and that is transportation. They have to buy buses, and one of these big buses costs a whole lot of money. And they have to pay the drivers and they have all kinds of other expenses. If everybody stole rides the way you are doing, there would be no more buses. You're getting this ride and you're going to pay for it. So go right up there to the driver and tell him you deliberately dodged him but that you have thought better of it. And hand him the fifteen cents."

The boy protested. "Aw gee, Dad, I'd look silly. I'm not going to do it."

"Oh yes, you are," the father insisted, "and if you don't I'll thrash you so hard you won't be able to sit down for a week. You've got to learn, even if the hard way, to do the right thing."

While the boy went cringingly up to make confession and restitution, I turned around and said admiringly to the father, "Well, I'm glad there's one left, a real, honest American father!"

When the boy returned the father affectionately punched him in the chest. Years from now, that kid will proudly boast of "my tough, honest old man."

Another thing that weakens people's inner restraints is

corruption in high places that goes unpunished. The other day my barber was talking bitterly about a certain government official whose misconduct had been the subject of a Senate investigation. There was plenty of adverse evidence, but in the end the whole messy affair was simply swept under the rug. With justification, taxpayers everywhere grumbled at this dishonesty, for every person who cheats the government is actually putting his slimy hand in your pocket and mine.

"The same day they voted to discontinue that investigation," my barber went on, "the government decided to disallow some exemptions I'd claimed on my income tax. This meant that I actually had to mortgage my home in order to pay up. How do you think I felt, seeing that crook get away with murder while I was being squeezed dry? I tell you, there are times when being honest just seems like a form of stupidity!"

I told him that I could not agree with that, but I did agree that dishonesty always breeds more dishonesty. Take the highly publicized sex antics of some of our movie stars, for example. Their glamorized adulteries make a mockery of marriage, and yet by and large they remain pampered, petted, idolized, famous, and rich. Subconsciously, at least, many people who find themselves facing the temptation to cheat on their husbands or wives must say to themselves, "Well, if these highly paid adulterers can get away with it, why shouldn't we?"

Thus the immoralities of a single individual can have deeply anti-social consequences by weakening the inner restraints of literally millions of people. And if enough people abandon their principles, they in turn add impetus to the moral decline by giving substance to the deadliest rationalization of all, namely, that wrongdoing must somehow be acceptable "because everybody's doing it."

It's in precisely this sort of vicious circle that our generation seems—at the moment—to be trapped. What is the answer?

To begin with, there is no swift or simple answer. The moral climate of a nation is a complex and massive thing. You can change it only by changing great numbers of people, and this takes time. The captain on the bridge of a gigantic ocean liner may decide in an emergency to change course, and may give the necessary orders, but the laws of inertia are working against him. It is only with agonizing slowness that the bow of the great ship finally begins to swing around. And when a nation gets off moral course, it isn't easy to get it back again.

Now it seems to me that if we are going to chart a new course away from the reefs and shoals of dishonesty, we are going to have to do three things.

First, we must convince people that dishonesty is not only a form of anarchy that can destroy society, it is also a kind of psychic poison that is extremely bad for them as human beings.

Next, we must make them understand that external forms of coercion—the laws, the police, and so on—can never do the job alone, that in the end it always comes down to the individual's free choice to act honestly or dishonestly. And we must make them feel the excitement and vitality and power and satisfaction that come from making the right choices.

Finally, we must show them how to evaluate their own performance in this all-important area of living, and how to improve it if it needs improving.

Let's begin by analyzing the effect that wrongdoing has on the wrongdoer himself.

Some years ago, visiting friends in Jamaica, I noticed an old map of that Caribbean island hanging on the wall. Across one barren and deserted area in the mountains ran a faint line of very small script. Looking closer, I was able to read it. It said: "The Land of Look-Behind." Intrigued, I asked my host what it meant.

"Oh," he said, "that map goes back to the days when there was still slavery here in Jamaica. When slaves escaped, as they sometimes did, they'd head for those mountains. Now and then the government would send troops in an effort to capture these poor runaways. So they must have spent a lot of time looking fearfully over their shoulders. And that's where the name came from. Rather romantic, isn't it? The Land of Look-Behind."

"To us, yes," I said. "To those poor souls, no. They might have escaped from the sugar plantations, but they were still slaves—slaves to fear. They had no real freedom. They were still wearing invisible chains."

"Invisible chains," my host repeated pensively. "You could probably make a sermon out of that."

Well, I never did make a sermon out of it, but some day I might, because the parallel is valid. People who choose dishonesty instead of honesty do go through life dragging invisible chains. Even when they stifle their consciences with rationalizations and excuses, something in them is always looking back fearfully, wondering if their wrongdoing is going to catch up with them. They can't live abundantly in the present, or look forward hopefully to the future. They are trapped in the Land of Look-Behind.

When you start looking into dishonesty in depth, you see once again that the Bible is right: the wages of sin *is* death —not physical extinction, necessarily, but a kind of psychic death that robs the victim of his life force in countless different ways. The casebooks of any psychiatrist are full of grim illustrations of this truth—example after example of people who defy their conscious conscience but whose *unconscious* conscience demands that they punish themselves in one way or another. Some are chronic accident victims, some commit senseless crimes just so that they will be arrested and punished, some demand the supreme penalty from themselves and attempt suicide.

As a minister, part of my job is to counsel with troubled individuals, and, believe me, I see endless examples of the ravages of suppressed guilt. I see what happens to people who suffer from their own dishonesty, even though nobody else may know. Once, I remember, after I had spoken in a New Jersey church, a woman sought me out and said, "What on earth is the matter with me? Everytime I go to church, I start itching terribly." She pushed up her sleeve and showed me a kind of rash on her arm. "Look at that. I almost go crazy sitting in the pew and trying to keep from scratching the life out of myself."

"Well," I said smiling, "I've had some odd reactions to my sermons, but this is something new."

"It's no joke," she said, and I could see that she was in deadly earnest. "I'm going to stop coming to church. I just can't stand it any longer."

I thought she might be allergic to the seat cushions, or some such thing. "Does this happen in other churches?" I asked her.

"Any church," she said. "Any church at all."

I asked if I might discuss the problem with her physician. She gave me permission, and I telephoned him. "This woman," said the doctor, "is suffering from what might be called internal eczema, she's mentally scratching herself on the inside. I haven't been able to get at the real cause of it. Actually, I don't think it's medical at all. Perhaps it's in your department."

This seemed possible, since the attacks of itching occurred only in church and might well be manifestations of an inflamed conscience. A lot of people believe they can fool their fellow man, and do, but fooling God and yourself is a little more difficult. Of course, you're under the eye of God at all times, whether you're in church or not. But some people seem to think God only takes a good look at them in church. This obviously is wrong. And another thing is equally certain; no matter how hard and fast you run, you can never get away from yourself. You always have you to deal with.

So I had some counseling sessions with this woman, and sure enough, I discovered that over the years, working as an accountant, she had been systematically stealing money from her employer. She told me, with tears, that she had begun with very small sums, that she always meant to pay it back, but that now it amounted to a good many thousands of dollars. It was an old and sadly familiar story.

As a spiritual doctor, I sometimes prescribe medicine that is hard to take, but it cures. I told her that there was only one possible course of action. She had to confess and she had to start paying the money back. Restitution, as much as is possible, is part of healing.

"But they'll fire me!" she sobbed.

"Maybe they will," I agreed. "But it's far better to lose a job than to lose your mind—or your soul."

In the end, she went to her employer and courageously confessed everything. And her boss did fire her. He said he had no choice. "But," he added, "since you have made this admission voluntarily, and since you say you'll pay the money back, I won't prosecute you. In fact, I'll give you a reference as a conscientious person—because only your conscience could have made you admit all this."

From that moment, the itch never troubled that woman again. It doesn't seem too farfetched to say that what she was really suffering from was an itch to do the right thing. And once she did it, the itch went away.

I believe that this "itch to do what's right" exists in all of us. My friend Dr. Clarence W. Leib, who helped me start the religio-psychiatric clinic in our church, told me of a patient he once had who suffered from all sorts of complaints —headaches, fatigue, tension, too-rapid pulse, gastric disturbances, and so on. None of the standard remedies had any effect. The unhappy man continued to haunt Dr. Leib's office. Finally the doctor told him that his troubles were caused by some powerful emotional pressure or conscience violation. He urged him to get whatever was bothering him out in the open.

At first the man insisted that his conscience was perfectly clear. But finally he broke down and confessed that he was defrauding his own brother. Their father had died a year or two before, leaving a large estate and naming this man executor. He had been arranging things so that his brother, who lived in Europe, was receiving far less than his just share.

Dr. Leib told the man—just as I told the woman with the itch—that only confession and restitution could make things right. The man protested frantically that he could never admit to his brother, who trusted him completely, the full extent of his duplicity and dishonesty. But finally, with Leib urging him on, he wrote a letter begging his brother's forgiveness and enclosing a large check as the first step in balancing the account.

Even then, Dr. Leib was afraid the man might falter in his resolve and not mail the letter. So he personally escorted him to a mail drop in the hall of the medical building. The man dropped the letter into the slot, took a deep breath, turned, and looked the doctor in the eye. "Thanks," he said. "I feel as if a terrible weight has been lifted off me. I feel good. I know I'm cured."

And he *was* cured. From that moment, all his symptoms left him. "Now you see," Dr. Leib told him gently, "you've been paying me money all these months to cure you when you could have been cured at any time for the price of one postage stamp!"

Make no mistake about it: any kind of dishonesty cripples you, and the first thing you lose is your freedom. A young man—let's say—persuades his girl friend to let him make love to her. After all, he tells her, people shouldn't be bound by the old moral codes, they should be free. But the irony is that, once they have taken this step, they are no longer free. They have risks that they did not have before. Even if the girl *doesn't* get pregnant, even if she's *not* tormented by uncertainty or guilt, she will find herself changed. She will be forced to conceal and rationalize and justify her behavior. She becomes a prisoner of her new "freedom."

Very often a person who had made a wrong decision—and knows it—will react with a kind of defiance, an I-don't-care attitude that is really camouflage for a deep uneasiness. Such a person will scoff at moral integrity or high principles in other people. There is a passage in the Bible that has always impressed me with its subtle wisdom, the first words of the Book of Psalms: *Blessed is the man who walketh not in the counsel of the ungodly, nor standeth in the way of sinners, nor sitteth in the seat of the scornful.* Now notice the progression outlined here. First the wrongdoer merely *walks* in wicked ways; the Bible implies that he is just passing through them, he still has a choice. Then he *stands* in the shadowy realm of immorality, the implication being that he has grown to like it and sees no reason for moving on. Finally he *sits,* stubbornly and defiantly, in the seat of the scornful and mocks those who are still attempting to do right.

This progression—or rather, regression—is no accident. If you deliberately violate your principles and make a wrong choice, that first decision is usually quite a struggle. As a matter of fact, a lot of people who make one such mistake never repeat it, because their conscience bothers them too much. But if you go on and make the mistake again and again, a kind of moral numbness creeps in until you no longer feel any twinges of remorse. And the final stage comes when you not only justify what you are doing but sneer at those who refuse to do it.

A year or two ago out in California a janitor found on the street a mail sack containing almost a quarter of a million dollars in cash. It had fallen, somehow, from an armored car carrying bank funds. He took it home, telephoned the F.B.I., and turned it in. His honesty brought him a reward and many letters of approval. But then, to his astonishment, angry, taunting letters began to pour in, berating him for being such a fool. People would call him on the phone and upbraid him furiously, as if his honesty was something that actually enraged them. In the end, to get away from these "sitters in the seat of the scornful," this man had to sell his home and move to another part of the city.

The point I am trying to make is a direct and brutal one, but any psychiatrist, any minister, any close observer of life will back me up. Sustained dishonesty will do one of two things to a person. Either it will make you physically sick, or it will leave you spiritually calloused. Either way, you are crippled. Either way, you are robbing yourself of the chance to live fully and joyously and abundantly. Either way you are hurting, not helping yourself.

My barber in his anger felt that only a fool would choose to be an honest man, but he was completely wrong. It is the dishonest man who is being the fool, because by being dishonest he is enslaving himself.

The second thing we have to hammer home where personal honesty is concerned is that in the end it always comes down to the individual's free choice. Christ Himself was always stressing this. In one of His parables, you remember, Jesus tells the story of a man who goes away on a journey. Before he goes, he entrusts a sum of money to each of his three servants. One man gets five talents, another two, and the third servant gets one.

Now what could indicate more clearly Christ's belief in the importance of individual responsibility? The master doesn't stay at home and supervise these servants. He doesn't set a detective to watch over them. He gives them complete freedom of choice and leaves them alone to exercise it as they see fit.

And what happens? The man with five talents puts the money to work and earns five talents more. The man with two talents does likewise. But the third man does nothing: afraid of making a mistake, he buries this talent in the ground. When the master comes home, he praises the first two servants for their initiative. But he calls the third man a "wicked and slothful servant," takes his talent away, and gives it to the servant with ten talents.

What if the first or second servant had made a bad investment? What if one or both had lost the money altogether? Would the master have condemned them also? I don't think so. I think he would have felt that they had the courage to try, that at least *they had made a choice*. The thing about the third servant that angered the master was his failure to accept responsibility, his failure to use the freedom of choice that was granted him.

This freedom of choice lies at the heart of all morality. It is not really the lock on the door or the policeman on the beat that prevents a burglar from breaking into a house—although they may be a deterrent. The choice is really up to the burglar, and all the forces of law and order in the world cannot get inside his skull and make up his mind for him. If his inner restraints do not restrain him, he is going to make the attempt . . . and it is the attempt that is immoral, regardless of whether it succeeds or fails.

Now, most of us never seriously contemplate burglary, but few of us are so insulated that we do not face and make moral choices all the time. And this is as it should be. If all the choices were made for us, if we were somehow compelled to do the right thing every time, there would be no great merit in our righteousness. It is precisely this freedom to do right or wrong that makes doing right an exhilarating and strengthening thing.

And it is exhilarating and strengthening. Have you ever been in a school where the honor system really works? You can feel the pride and the power in the atmosphere, and sense the dismay and anger when someone violates the code. Once, in such a school, I heard a skeptic say to the principal, "But this honor system is just asking for trouble. It gives the students a perfect opportunity to cheat!" "No," said the principal with a smile, "it gives them the opportunity *not* to cheat."

That schoolmaster was not just an optimist—he was also a shrewd observer of human nature. Just as deliberate wrongdoing loads a person with invisible chains of guilt, so conscious rightdoing liberates creative energy. I came across a vivid illustration of this the other day. A writer I know, a specialist in medical articles for popular magazines, told me that he received in his mail a check for $1500 from the public relations representative of a large pharmaceutical company. The public relations man wanted the writer to mention favorably the products of his company. He said that if this could be arranged, other checks would follow.

"Well, you know," the writer said to me, "the silly thing about all this was that I was occasionally mentioning this fellow's products quite legitimately. So he was trying to bribe me to do something I was already doing. And believe me, I needed the money. But somehow I couldn't quite bring myself to cash the check. It lay on my desk, day after day, and my work went very badly. Finally, somewhere, I found the courage to send it back. I knew that if I kept it I would be selling my independence and my integrity. And this was something I couldn't afford to do."

"And did your work go better?" I asked him.

He laughed. "It was fantastic. I was so pleased with myself and my decision that it was just as if a big wave of energy came out of nowhere and gave my typewriter wings. In less than a week, I wrote two complete articles—and made almost as much money anyway!"

Of course he did! He had made the right choice. He had won a victory, and something in him knew it, and his pride and confidence in himself as a human being spilled over into his work and made it sing.

I meet many people in my travels around the world, and I have often been struck by the fact that many highly successful people seem to live by what might be called a code of super-honesty. They're not satisfied with casual, everyday standards. They go an extra mile. They make the unusual choice. Take Johnny Mercer, for instance, one of the most successful songwriters of our time. When he was a boy growing up in Savannah, Georgia, his father's business failed. No dishonesty was involved; it just failed, and the investors lost all their money. Johnny went on to Hollywood and eventually had great success. By now his father had died, and the old debts were long since forgotten. But one day a banker in Savannah had a call from Johnny in Hollywood. Would he please look up all the stockholders in his father's business and see that everyone got his investment back, to the last penny? The banker was astounded, those old debts amounted to thousands of dollars. But Johnny quietly insisted that every one of them be paid. And they were.

Was Johnny Mercer the poorer for this transaction? Of course not. If anything, his talent burned brighter than ever. I thought of this as I watched him on television getting another Oscar—not too long ago. And I had a feeling that somewhere his father might be watching him too, with the kind of love and pride that no amount of money can buy.

Lots of empire-builders have this sense of super-honesty. J. Arthur Rank, the great English film producer, always asks himself one question before he makes a decision. Not "Is this potentially profitable?" or "Will it be a success?" but simply "Is it right?" It doesn't matter whether the decision involves six million pounds or sixpence; he always subjects it to that test. An old wholesale grocer I once knew in Syracuse, New York, Harlowe B. Andrews, had the same approach. "Be sure that what you do is right," Brother Andrews would say, "because if it isn't right, it's wrong, and no wrong ever turned out right!" This was the way he ran his business. And, I might add, he sold a lot of groceries!

Now, I'm not trying to imply that if you always do the right thing you will always get rich, or that the universe automatically hands out celestial lollipops to good little girls and boys. But it stands to reason that if a person has a clear conscience, if he doesn't have to waste time telling lies designed to cover up earlier lies or waste energy trying to conceal or justify dubious practices, if he has the confidence that comes from meeting moral issues squarely, then he is going to function a lot more efficiently than a person who lives on the shady side of the street.

There is something almost tangible about complete honesty, complete integrity. When you encounter it in a person you know it, and you know you can trust him. This ability to inspire trust and confidence is often a factor in their success. Take the case of my friend Ruth Hardy of Palm Springs, California. For over twenty years, until she died recently, Ruth operated the Ingleside Inn, a beautiful place at the foot of the mountains on the edge of the desert. In her last years, things went extremely well for Ruth, but this wasn't always the case. When her marriage broke up a quarter of a century ago, she found herself saddled with crushing debts. She could have gone through bankruptcy, no doubt, but instead she wrote to each of her creditors offering them a choice: she would pay half the amount due immediately, or ten dollars a month until the whole debt was liquidated.

Every single creditor elected to take the half payment, doubtless thinking that half a loaf was better than none. So, legally, that left Ruth in the clear. But several years later, when she began to get ahead, she went to each of her creditors, who had long since written off the debt, and voluntarily paid the other half. "It was the right thing to do," she told me. "Not doing it would have upset me, slowed me down, made me doubt my own integrity. You'll never get anywhere if you're a poor credit risk with yourself!"

Ruth knew something about that aspect of things, too. When she purchased an old home with spacious grounds in Palm Springs, and decided to turn it into a hotel, the banks refused to lend her money. It was impossible, they told her, to make a small, American-plan hotel pay. When she went ahead anyway, her suppliers also made her pay cash because they too believed that her venture would collapse. Eventually she became one of the best credit risks in her community. She served twelve years on the city council and twice was offered the office of mayor. Her prescription for success was simple: "Put your life in God's hands," she said, "ask Him for guidance, work hard, and *do what you think is right*. There's a lot of power in that formula. It really works."

What she meant was the quiet power that comes to people who face up to moral issues—and make the right choice.

The third thing we need to teach people is the importance of honest self-appraisal. After all, you are the only one —probably—who knows exactly where you stand morally. You're the only one who can decide to raise your standards higher. Suppose you do decide to strengthen your moral muscles and gain the corresponding rewards. Are there specific things you can do?

Yes, there are half a dozen specific things that anyone can do. Let's consider them, one by one, in the next chapter.

MEMO TO THE READER NO. 2

"Take Ten"

I must say, I've always felt indebted to the man who invented the literary device known as the chapter. I don't know who he was, but he had a great idea. A new chapter gives a writer a wonderful feeling of excitement and buoyancy and optimism. Here's a new chance to say something and—hopefully—say it better. It's a great device for the reader, too. He has time to catch his breath. He can close the book, think about what he has read. He can even go away, attend to other things, then come back, find his place easily, and resume his friendship with the writer.

This rhythm of concentration followed by relaxation runs all through life. After all, each day in itself is a new chapter, a new challenge. We have learned in industry that the coffee break doesn't interfere with productivity—it increases it. Even in something as intense as a rehearsal for a play, the time comes when the director has to call a halt, tell his actors to take time out, relax for a few minutes. "Take Ten."

So let's "Take Ten" in our discussion of the erosion of honesty, and see where we stand and where we're going. We've talked about the prevalence of dishonesty which is a sign of the times, bleak proof that people are discarding the old external restraints without substituting inner controls. We've pointed out the damage that dishonesty can do to the dishonest person, the chains of guilt, the physical and spiritual maladjustment that it brings. We've emphasized the freedom of choice that each of us has, and the feeling of exhilaration and strength and power that comes from making the right choices.

Now it's time to discuss specific things that each of us can do to make ourselves more honest than we are. And this really deserves a new chapter, because it requires some thought and effort and self-honesty.

Some chapters you can read quickly; others you can read slowly; still others you should read twice.

Maybe this next chapter is one you should read twice!

CHAPTER III

Blow the Dust off Your Standards

If the preceding pages have left you convinced that honesty really is the best policy, what should you do about it? If you want to raise the moral standards of your community, or your nation, or the world, what do you do?

The answer to that is simple: you begin with yourself. And here are six things to do, starting today.

1. *Take a moral inventory.* This is not so easy as it sounds. Most of us are accustomed to thinking of ourselves as rather admirable people, and we're not exactly anxious to have this happy conviction shaken. But if you turn a bright and searching light on your daily conduct, you are probably going to find areas of shadow here and there.

You might begin by asking yourself, with grim honesty, whether your moral standards are higher or lower than they were five years ago. Do you now condone things—on the grounds of liberalism or sophistication—that you would have condemned in your more idealistic days? Have you become so accustomed to *little* distortions of the truth, to *minor* acts of dishonesty, that you are hardly aware of them any more?

Sometimes it helps to review with ruthlessness your moral performance in the chief areas of living—your job, your marriage, your social life, your relationship with your children.

Take your job, for example. You probably wouldn't dream of stealing merchandise. But do you ever steal time? Do you ever come in late, leave early, stretch out coffee breaks, prolong conversations in the rest room? You probably wouldn't dream of stealing money, either. But do you ever pad an expense account, or charge a private long-distance call to the company? What ethically, is the difference?

Call yourself on the carpet. Answer yes or no. Discard all those weak-kneed rationalizations such as, "Well, everybody does it." Get these little grains of sand out of your moral gears!

And remember that sometimes your obligations to yourself and your fellow man transcend your obligations to your job. Two or three years ago a friend of mine who lives in a university town in the South told me that men of good will in his community had done a quiet but effective job of preparing the student body for the integration of the college. But on the day that the first Negro students were to enroll, a group of reporters and television cameramen appeared. Finding no agitation or disturbance, they did their best to create the semblance of one. "Can't you just clench your fist here in front of the camera?" one white student was asked. "Here's a microphone; tell us how you really feel about all this!" a reporter cried. Fortunately, the students ignored them. But those men were not reporting the news, they were trying to create it. They were practicing dishonesty on a fundamental level, out of an easy rationalization that it was their job to report news.

What about your marriage? Are there areas in your life —or even in your thoughts—where you deceive your marriage partner? What about your social life? Are you always loyal to your friends? Isn't plain, everyday gossip usually a form of malicious exaggeration—in other words, dishonesty? What about your children? Do you always tell them the truth? Do you set up standards for them that you refuse to meet yourself?

If you do take a searching moral inventory of yourself, you will find many apparently harmless little areas of deception. An unwelcome telephone call comes to your office. "Oh, tell him I'm out!" you say to your secretary. Someone whose name and face you can't recall comes up to you on the street. "Remember meeting me?" they say. "Oh, yes," you assure them, groping desperately for some clue as to where or when. Do these small lapses from the truth affect your regard for it in more important things? I think perhaps they do. In my own case, I know, I have tried to eliminate them simply as a form of self-discipline.

There is even such a thing as conversational dishonesty. Do you ever find yourself wavering from your own convictions and saying things that you think your listeners want to hear? If you do, you have plenty of company! For example, the other day I was in the office of an elderly friend of mine who is a very successful industrialist. He told me that recently he had had a visit from quite a prominent bishop who was hoping to persuade him to contribute a large sum to some worthy cause or other. "But he didn't get it," my friend said a bit grimly.

I was surprised. "Why not?"

"Because," said my outspoken old friend, "he's a crook, that's why!"

"Oh, come now," I said, "the bishop's ideas on some topics may be a bit different from yours or mine, but he's hardly a crook!"

"Well," he said, "in my book a dishonest person is a crook, and he's not honest. When he asked for an appointment with me, I took the trouble to read some of his pronouncements and sermons in which he expressed some ideas with which I disagree. Then, when he arrived, I asked his opinion on some of those same questions. And he didn't tell me what he really believed. He told me what he thought I wanted to hear, what he thought would put me in a good humor. So I say he's a crook, and I didn't give him a nickel!"

The moral is crystal clear. Honesty *is* the best policy, even for bishops.

2. *Find and use a moral yardstick.* "Behind a great deal of our modern immorality," writes my distinguished colleague Harry Emerson Fosdick, "is not so much downright badness as sincere confusion as to what is right." Well, maybe this is true in some instances, although it seems a pretty fine distinction to me. But when such confusion exists, I'm sure it arises because the individual tries to make all moral judgment for himself, studiously avoiding the guidelines that already exist.

This is a good deal like going on a journey into unknown territory and refusing to take either a compass or a map. In the first place, your own judgment in deciding a moral issue is often clouded by emotion or personal considerations. In the second place, why go to all that bother when the time-tested wisdom of the profoundest minds in history is already at your disposal?

The great moral yardsticks that religion offers are the Ten Commandments and the Golden Rule. Philosophers of all ages have tried to improve on them, without much success. The great German thinker, Immanuel Kant, offered as a guide to morals his Categorical Imperative: always act as if your action could become a universal principle to be used by all men. Yet what is this but the Golden Rule in fancy clothing?

Some people I know find a moral yardstick in this question: "What would Jesus do?" Certainly if you apply that standard conscientiously to any contemplated action you will not go wrong. One man told me, wryly, that he has a less lofty but very effective way of checking on the rightness or wrongness of a given action: he visualizes his role as if reported in big black headlines in the next day's newspaper. If something in him winces at the thought, he tells himself he had better review the situation. Admittedly there is something droll about an imaginary news story beginning: "This week Mary Jones of 21 Elm Street stole only $1.85 worth of postage stamps from her employer instead of the usual $2.25." But it's an effective little mental trick, all the same.

So if you don't have a moral yardstick, get one. And if you do have one, blow the dust off it and start measuring again!

3. *Use thought-control.* All actions, good or bad, start with a thought. If you can block the thought that leads to a dishonest deed, you will block the deed itself, because you break the chain of cause-and-effect that leads to the deed.

A psychiatrist once told me of a married man who came to him with a problem. He was having an affair with another woman. And something in him wanted to break off with her. But he admitted that he couldn't do it. "I make good resolutions," he said. "But once I'm with her I forget them all."

The psychiatrist asked him where he met the woman, and learned that it was at her apartment. It was one of those apartments where the caller presses a button, and the occupant of the apartment presses another one that releases the lock of the door leading in from the street.

"You say you can't keep your resolutions once you're with this woman," said the psychiatrist. "I believe you. But are you strong enough to keep from pressing a button?"

The man said that he thought he was.

"All right," said the psychiatrist. "When you find yourself standing in front of that door, put your hands in your pockets and keep them there. Don't press that button. Concentrate every ounce of your *won't*-power on not touching it. You say you want to break these chains that are holding you. All right, break them at the weakest link."

The man managed to do this once or twice—and the evil spell was broken. He called up the woman and told her he was through with her.

It would also help if people contemplating some form of wrongdoing would look past the deed itself to its possible, or even probable consequences. This sort of hindsight-in-advance would save a lot of grief and trouble in this world. In one of his books, to illustrate this point, Thomas Carlyle tells the story of a man with murder in his heart and a pistol in his hand. His intended victim stands before him; his finger tightens on the trigger. Now if, in that split second, he decides to pull the trigger, his entire life will be changed. Nothing will put things back the way they were. No remorse will save him from the consequences. As Omar Khayyám put it:

> The moving finger writes; and having writ,
> Moves on: nor all your piety nor wit
> Shall lure it back to cancel half a line,
> Nor all your tears wash out a word of it.

In this realm of morals, what the moving finger writes is up to you. If people would just stop to think of the endless consequences that one wrong decision can have, they would be a lot less likely to leap before they look.

4. *Speak out.* The fourth thing you can do to strengthen your own standards of honesty is to speak out forcibly against dishonesty wherever you come into contact with it. Too many of us have a tendency to condone things by keeping silent. We're afraid we'll be disliked if we object. We fear we may be considered smug or self-righteous.

If you make a habit of being easy on wrongdoers, you are likely to wind up being too easy on yourself. On the other hand, if you speak out loud and clear in favor of honesty, you make it difficult for yourself to be anything but honest . . . unless you are a hopeless hypocrite.

I always admire my wife Ruth for the quiet but firm way in which she makes known her stand on an ethical problem. The last time we were in Hong Kong, we went shopping for gifts to bring home. The shopkeeper offered to write up a receipt listing wholesale prices, not the prices we actually paid. This way, he said, we could fool the customs officials, buy more things, and still be under our allowance. Ruth told him, in polite but final tones, to make out the receipts correctly. She was not going to be party to any scheme, however minor, to defraud our own government.

Ruth is probably the most even-tempered person I know. She almost never raises her voice to anyone. But not long ago I saw her get very angry—with a pious fraud.

Now the worst kind of fraud, I think, is the sanctimonious one who tries to camouflage his wrongdoing with saccharine references to the brotherhood of man or pious appeals to the Almighty. The gentleman in this case, an ordained minister, had been entrusted with some funds for a specific purpose. And he had, to put it bluntly, appropriated them for his own use. When Ruth and I confronted him with this, he did not deny it, but tried to explain his dishonesty in pious weasel words.

"What are you going to do about it?" we demanded.

"It's a very difficult situation," he sighed. "Perhaps we should pray together about it."

My gentle and mild-mannered wife gave him a steely look. "Mr. So-and-so," she said, "what you are saying is an affront to Almighty God. You have mishandled money, and until you pay it back I shall pray only that you become an honest man and not a phony. Let's hear no more insincere pious talk!"

The man went away looking like a chastened small boy, and eventually he did pay the money back. Just as there is power in goodness, there is power in righteous indignation, too. So don't be afraid to smite the dragon of dishonesty whenever you encounter it. Hearing you, other people may take heart—and certainly something in you will be purified and strengthened.

Sometimes you have to do more than merely speak out—you have to take decisive action. All too often people seem to be paralyzed when confronted with criminal acts of injustice or violence. Something in them turns away. They just don't want to get involved.

But not always. Just the other day I heard of a man who did not turn away. His name is Sal Lazzarotti; he is Art Director of *Guideposts* Magazine. And what happened to him shows how faith in the right, supported by the teachings of Holy Scripture, can give a man strength to involve himself in the troubles of others.

Sal commutes to his New York office by subway. One morning he observed a lanky, dark-haired boy, about eighteen, standing by the center post. Directly across from Sal sat an attractive young lady—a brunette, perhaps twenty-five—reading a paper-back book. As the train pulled to a stop at the next station, the brunette arose and walked toward the door, passing the dark-haired boy. Suddenly, she whirled and screamed: "You fresh punk! Can't you keep your hands off people! Don't look so innocent. I know what you did!"

Then the girl began hitting the astonished boy. In self-defense he threw up his hands and tried to push her away. One hand struck her face—suddenly there was blood on her mouth.

The boy dashed out of the subway car and down the platform. The girl followed—her high heels clicking as she ran. "Police! Police!" she screamed.

The doors of the subway car closed. As the train rumbled on to the next station, passengers shrugged their shoulders and returned to their newspapers and books.

Sal sat there perplexed. He had been watching the boy and had detected no move to touch the girl. He wondered what would happen to the boy if he were caught. He guessed the girl's story would carry more weight. "It's not your affair," Sal told himself. "Don't stick your nose in someone else's business. Besides, he probably got away and nothing will come of it."

At the office, Sal got to work. But he could not forget what had taken place. Finally, he picked up the telephone.

It took four calls for Sal to locate the right police precinct. The desk sergeant listened to his story. "You saw it all, huh? Well, the boy has been sent to Juvenile Court, downtown. Call there if you want to help him."

Sal had a full schedule of work. He had no time to be a witness in a court case. He remembered a story he had read recently about a man rushing to help a screaming girl in a car; the man ended up in prison on an assault charge because he tried to stop her attacker. Sal told himself: "This thing could boomerang on me."

But one timeless truth and example kept nudging him: Jesus and the story of the Good Samaritan kept coming to mind. It would not leave him at peace.

Sal called Juvenile Court and discovered the boy's name—Steve Larsen—and his home address. Soon he was talking to his mother who sobbed that she had no money to hire a lawyer.

Sal located a lawyer who agreed to represent the boy without charge. He talked with the lawyer; he talked with the boy.

The hearing was set for Monday morning. The boy's mother arrived and sat down in the courtroom with Sal and the lawyer. Then Steve Larsen was brought in. Sal learned that if convicted, the boy would receive six months to a year in jail. The judge came into the room and proceedings began. The Assistant District Attorney presented the girl's charges, then the judge began questioning her.

Without hesitation, with great positiveness, she described what Steve had supposedly done. Sal shook his head in disbelief. Nothing she said could possibly have happened.

Finally, the judge interrupted, asking her to be more specific: "There is a witness to the incident present, so be sure of what you say . . ."

The girl's eyes searched the room and came to rest on Sal. She looked at him incredulously. She resumed her testimony, but started fumbling with words, qualifying previous statements and contradicting herself.

Within five minutes, the judge called the lawyer and the prosecutor forward. They huddled, whispered, and nodded. Then the boy's lawyer returned with a grin on his face. "The case has been dismissed," he said. "The judge feels the girl needs psychiatric help."

And so an innocent boy was saved from a prison term and a blot that could have ruined his life—all because one man was not afraid to involve himself with a person in need.

5. *Be prepared for some moments of loneliness.* There are times when the path of righteousness can seem the loneliest place in the world. Many of the greatest figures of history have discovered this. Socrates, when they brought him the hemlock. Lincoln, sitting alone in the White House while his commanders lost battle after battle in the field. And think of the loneliness that Jesus felt in the Garden of Gethsemane when He asked His closest and most beloved friends to watch with Him while He prayed for strength to endure the ordeal that lay ahead—and twice came back from His agony and found them sleeping.

But what you have to remember, when such loneliness comes upon you, is that you are not really alone. God is with you. If your loneliness is the result of some difficult but honorable choice, He knows about it, and loves you for it. Not only that, there are always people who admire right-doing and support it in their hearts, even though they are silent.

I knew a girl once, a very shy, almost timid girl who worked in a factory. She was a member of a labor union that was gradually being infiltrated by Communists. This became more and more apparent to her as she sat in union meetings. Yet no member of the rank-and-file seemed to be aware of the danger, or interested in doing anything about it.

The thought of speaking out filled this girl with terror. But one day she could stand it no longer. Trembling, she stood up in the meeting and voiced her suspicions and fears. She looked around for support—and there was none. Just bent heads and closed faces and an apprehensive silence. She thought she had failed, completely and utterly. And she felt so alone that she could barely keep from bursting into tears.

But she wasn't alone. After the meeting, hesitantly, almost furtively, six other union members came up to her, praised her for her courage, told her they agreed with her. These seven people got together quietly and decided to organize anti-Communist cells inside the union. They actually borrowed Communist techniques of infiltration and turned them against the Communists. The end of the story was that the Communist takeover was blocked. And all because one person had the courage to speak out and endure the loneliness —the awful, though temporary loneliness—of being in the right.

6. *Demand the highest ethical performance of yourself.* In an age where external controls have grown weak or are actually disappearing, the individual must set up his own standards and must set them high—this is the theme of this book. And only you, as an individual, can do it. The preacher can preach, the writer can write, the moralist can exhort. But nothing will happen unless the individual says to himself, I *choose.* I choose the higher path. I choose the more difficult goal. Of my own free will, I choose it. "Choose you

this day," says the Bible, "whom ye will serve." Will it be good, or will it be evil?

If standards fall too low, nations perish . . . this seems to be a natural law. If nations are to survive, somebody must keep the standards high. I remember a story that J. P. McEvoy, a *Reader's Digest* roving editor, used to tell about the time he went to London and decided to visit an English court of law to observe British justice in action. The case being tried was one of wife-beating, with the wife as chief witness. She graphically described her husband's brutality, but at the last minute had a change of heart. "I wish to withdraw my complaint, your Lordship," she said to the judge. "I find no fault with this man." His Lordship looked grimly down from the bench. "England does!" he said, and proceeded to pass sentence anyway.

Inside each of us, I believe, sits a monitor just as intolerant of evil as that English judge. His name is Conscience and we must take care not to stifle his voice or blunt the edge of his sense of justice. For, as wise men have held through the ages, the voice of Conscience is very close to the voice of God.

If, then, we reject dishonesty as unworthy and enervating, if we choose goodness not just for its own sake but because of the power that it gives us, if we examine ourselves closely and resolve to raise our standards higher, we shall not only be helping ourselves, we shall be helping the world along the upward path of evolution. Or, to use the old Biblical phrase, we shall be drawing closer to the kingdom of God.

MEMO TO THE READER NO. 3

The Dubious Power of "Don't"

Now and then in my mail I get a letter that makes me stop and think. I got one yesterday. It was from an exasperated teenager who took exception to a sermon he had just sat through. "We young people," he wrote, "are fed up with lectures on morality. And do you know why? Because they just consist of an endless series of Don'ts. It's always, 'Don't do this! Don't do that! Don't do anything.' And we're sick of it."

Well, you know, I think that angry young man has a point. Too often morality *is* made to seem like a gloomy procession of negatives. It's made to seem like a minus rather than a plus.

The trouble with this approach is that the power of "Don't" is really limited in many areas. Take the matter of cigarette smoking, for example. In the past few years, overwhelming evidence has been presented pointing to the conclusion that cigarette smoking is a major health menace, conducive not only to lung cancer but to a host of other physical ills. Smoking cigarettes is plainly unwise and dangerous, and a chorus of voices has arisen—all saying "Don't!" Doctors say "Don't"; insurance companies say "Don't"; countless magazine articles say "Don't." And what happens? People go right on smoking; *because purely negative arguments will not stop them*. The only thing that will ever stop them is an inner conviction, made by themselves, within themselves, for positive reasons leading to positive action. They will not listen if you say, "Don't smoke; it's bad for you." They might listen if someone said, "Why not control your life, why not be the master of your habits, why not know the excitement and pride and joy of self-responsibility and self-command?"

No doubt there is a streak of human contrariness at work here. Being told not to do something strikes a perverse spark of defiance in many of us. We are much more likely to

47

heed a command to do something than an order to refrain from doing something. "Help us grow this grass" is a more effective sign than simply "Keep off the grass." Jesus Christ emphasized this truth when He took the old Hebraic rule of conduct, "Do *not* to others that which you do *not* wish done to you" and converted it into the Golden Rule.

The great trouble with the "Don't" approach to human affairs, it seems to me, is that it fails to allow for growth on the part of the individual. It gives him fixed boundaries, but it also hems him in. If the rules are too rigid, if the area for growth is too restricted, then the individual must either resign himself to not growing, or he must break through the barriers. Thus in a maturing society, as in a maturing individual, too-rigid authority leads, in the end, to defiance of authority.

I have watched this happen in my own lifetime. As a small boy, growing up in various rural Ohio towns, I lived in a society hedged about by rules. It was a good life, and it produced good people, but looking back now I believe that the list of "Don'ts" was too inclusive. It was not just "Don't drink" or "Don't smoke," prohibitions that were and are valid for many good reasons. It was also "Don't play cards" and "Don't dance" and "Don't go to the theater" and "Don't do anything enjoyable on Sunday." We lived under a form of Puritanism, really, stern and well-intentioned, but also naïve. Cards were equated with gambling, and dancing with orgies, and the theater meant vice and fallen women. As late as the turn of the century, a student was actually expelled from my college, Ohio Wesleyan, for going to see a Shakespearean play. Anything as repressive and narrow-minded as this was bound to bring about a rebellion against purely negative rules. And it did. We are living in the midst of that rebellion right now.

And so I should like to offer a suggestion: when you are trying to outline the rules of living for your children—or even for yourself—don't rely too heavily on "Don't." When there are negative reasons for not doing something, there are often positive reasons for doing the reverse. Seek for these, find your motivation in them, and you will come much closer to your goal.

I'm not saying—or even hinting—that all "Don'ts" can be eliminated. Obviously they can't. Christ Himself did not try to reinterpret or change the Ten Commandments, which for the most part are tremendous "Don'ts." But Christ did add the positive commandment to love—to love God and your fellow man.

Down through the ages, some of the most thunderous "Don'ts" leveled at mankind have had to do with sex. This is not surprising, because sex is just about the most powerful and explosive force that is built into us. There is plenty of evidence, all around us, that where sex is concerned, the old repressive, authoritarian controls are breaking down. It's a very serious situation. In the next section of this book, therefore, let's examine it and see what can be done about it.

CHAPTER IV

The Whirlwinds of Sex

In my office sits a sobbing young woman. She is about thirty, quite pretty, married, with two children. She is weeping with remorse and regret, and perhaps with relief. Confession is good for the soul, and she has had a lot to confess. She has told me her story, and ended it with two questions. "What's wrong with me, Dr. Peale? What's wrong with the world?"

Those questions seem to hang in the quiet air. Outside, dimly, I can hear the roar of the traffic along Fifth Avenue. Here in the office, as so often before, I seem to hear the clamor of a confused and sorrowing human heart.

Her story in itself is not so unusual. Any social worker, any minister who does not live in an ivory tower, would be familiar with it. A young married couple, sophisticated, gay, a little bored with each other and with suburban life. Add half a dozen other similar couples. Mix frequently with alcohol and "emancipated" ideas about sex. An affair begins in the group which soon becomes a matter of general discussion. What's sauce for the goose is sauce for the gander. The little evil core of promiscuity spreads. Having an affair becomes a sort of dubious status symbol . . . if you aren't having one, you're not really keeping up with the Joneses. And so she gets involved. Only her conscience is not so elastic as she thought it was. She wants to end it; the man does not. Sleeplessness. Guilt. Erosion of emotional stability. Thoughts of self-destruction, so terrifying in themselves that she has been driven here, like a leaf caught up in a whirlwind and blown by chance through the open door of the church and into this quiet sanctuary.

What does the spiritual counselor feel at a moment like this? Not condemnation; it is too late for that. Pity, certainly. A desire to help, to restore, to rebuild. Love for this suffering, penitent human being. Awareness, too, of one's

50

own fallibility. The counselor doesn't have all the answers. He can't play God. He can only ask God to help him help the person who needs help.

"What's wrong with me, Dr. Peale? What's wrong with the world?" I know what is wrong with the young woman, all right. To use the blunt and old-fashioned term, she has sinned; she has broken the ancient and inflexible moral laws of God and man, and she is suffering the consequences. In a way, I am glad that she has this capacity for suffering; it shows that her conscience is far from dead; it proves that she still has a sense of right and wrong. And the pain she is feeling may be a necessary prelude to self-forgiveness. When we do something that we know is wrong, something in us chalks up the debt, and that debt must be paid, one way or another, before the books can be balanced.

But her self-condemnation must not progress to the point where she can no longer fulfill her role as a wife and mother. Somehow she must be helped to see that mistakes are not final or irrevocable, that the future can and will be better than the past. She needs a friendly hand to help her out of the quicksands into which she has fallen, help her back into the path of successful living.

And so I tell her of the gentleness with which Jesus treated the woman taken in adultery. I repeat His words to her: "Neither do I condemn thee: go, and sin no more." I tell her that many people are caught in these particular quicksands; that she is not the only one. I tell her quietly but firmly that she must end her relationship with the man who is not her husband, and that if she cannot bring herself to do it, I will call him on the telephone and do it for her. She straightens her shoulders and says she will do it herself, and I believe her. It is what the moral side of her wanted anyway, and now that she is no longer alone with her problem she will have the strength to do it.

Then, as she grows calmer, we talk about the background of her case, the underlying problems and pressures. She listens as I talk about the tidal wave of confusion that seems to have swept over the country where sex is concerned. She does not deny my suggestion that perhaps behind her wild and senseless behavior there was a desperate search for real meaning in her life, for deeper communication, that in some twisted and mistaken way it was a spiritual hunger that she was trying to satisfy in this bleak and sterile manner. She does not reject my further suggestion that religion would satisfy this hunger, if only she would let it.

And so, in the end, she goes away closing the door quietly behind her, and I am left to reflect on the power and prevalence of these whirlwinds of sex that sweep through people's lives, wrecking some, damaging others. How ironic that one of God's greatest gifts to man should be so deadly and destructive when misused. How ironic that in this enlightened age of spaceships and medical miracles we should be less wise in this crucial area of living than our fathers or our grandfathers. How ironic—and how sad!

From the beginning, in thinking and planning for this book, I knew I would have to write one chapter—probably two—on what has come to be known as the sex revolution. At the heart of every upward trend in human affairs lies a good idea, an inner core of rightness that provides the lift and the impetus and the thrust. Conversely, at the center of every negative and destructive trend you will find a dark area that poisons everything and that must be corrected before the blight can be removed. I believe the decline in moral standards all around us has such a core of evil. I think it lies in our obsession with—and misuse of—sex.

I also knew that these chapters would not be easy to write. Sex is a topic of universal interest, but around it swirl such powerful emotions and prejudices that a sane and balanced discussion of it is rare, to say the least. At one extreme there are people who feel that if you discuss the sex revolution at all you are condoning it—and, I must say, some of our self-appointed "sexperts" seem to be doing just that. At the other extreme are those, especially young people, who are convinced in advance that if a minister opens his mouth on the subject, he will (a) adopt a helpless and pious oh-isn't-it-awful attitude that will bore and exasperate them, (b) utter a series of thunderous prohibitions based on ancient authorities that no longer make sense to them, or (c) pontificate at length on a subject about which, being a minister, he is not likely to know very much.

But I am going to try it anyway, because I think that despite all that has been said and written the situation still calls urgently for clarification and correction. The plain truth is, in this tangled and difficult area of living, more and more people are finding themselves in trouble and in need of help. Here again, as I have pointed out before in this book, we have clamored for freedom from rules, we have cast off the bonds of authority, we have demanded liberty of expression and action. And what has happened? We have gotten our freedom, we have achieved our liberty —and we don't know what to do with them.

Look at what has happened. We relax our codes of censorship and our newsstands become clogged with filth. We encourage freedom of expression in our theater and the stage reeks with perversion. We suggest to young people that moral standards, after all, may not be absolute, that they may change with changing circumstances, and the rate of forced marriages and illegitimate births skyrockets. We say to our adult citizens, never mind the rules, just control yourselves and behave decently—only to find that the whirlwinds of sex are too powerful in many cases to yield to self-control.

This grim state of affairs is not the product of my imagination. The evidence is all around us; you would have to be an ostrich, with your head firmly embedded in the sand, not to see it. Still, not wanting to rely solely on my own observations, before sitting down to write these chapters I did some extensive research. I read literally dozens of books, pamphlets, magazine articles, sociological studies, statistical reports, and church pronouncements on both sides of the Atlantic. And I can assure you that it is impossible to expose yourself to such a cross section of fact and opinion without becoming chillingly convinced that what you are really studying is a grave disorder in the character and society of our nation—perhaps in the character of Western civilization itself. Many of our best thinkers are deeply disturbed by this. In a recent magazine article the celebrated novelist and Nobel Prize-winner Pearl S. Buck observed that, with the possible exception of the Chinese Communists, no people in the world have changed so much in the last twenty years as we Americans. "Nowhere," she added, "is the change more apparent than in our ethics of sex. The change is so abrupt and far-reaching that we are all dazed by it."

Abrupt is the right word. Most radical social changes come slowly. But not this time. It is almost as if the demonic powers in sex—and make no mistake, sex has its demonic side—had been released in a sudden explosion that has blasted away the restraints and traditions of centuries. The spark that has set off this explosion is a twisted concept of freedom, a "new freedom" that too often leaves its adherents in chains. Here is a distinguished educator speaking. He is Dean Robert E. Fitch of the Pacific School of Religion. "Young people today are losing control of their lives. They are having babies when they don't want them. They are getting married before they really want to. They are taking jobs before they are really prepared for them. And this is 'the new freedom'!" He goes on to point out that freedom is precisely what is being lost. "There is pathos in the life of anyone who has cheated himself of the freedom really to choose to get married, to choose to have a baby, to choose to take a job."

There is more than pathos in such lives; there is stark tragedy. As I write, a picture comes into my mind of a small, furnished room in a small Midwestern town. In it is a girl, sixteen years old, waiting to have some boy's illegitimate baby. She has left her own hometown in an effort to spare her parents shame and humiliation. They are helping her—at a distance. What are her thoughts every morning when she awakens, lonely and frightened and sick at soul? How does she face the empty, accusing day? What sort of agony will wring her soul when her baby comes and she has to give it away, perhaps without ever holding it or seeing it? This girl is just a statistic, true—every year there are at least a quarter of a million such babies born in our nation, and a million more who are not allowed to be born because abortionists make sure that they are not. But this girl, this statistic, happens to be the daughter of people I know, and the granddaughter of a clergyman. Multiply this one not-very-unusual case by tens of thousands and you have a reservoir of human agony that is unimaginable.

Yet many people will not face up to what is happening. Not long ago I attended a conference in a southern town where a sociologist drew a somber picture of the sexual chaos around us. He documented it with even more somber statistics. His audience listened attentively. But they acted as if they were hearing a report on conditions on Mars, or somewhere equally remote. "Our youngsters aren't like that," I heard them saying afterward. "They're fine, churchgoing kids."

Well, no doubt many of them are. But it is also possible that some parents are like the three monkeys determined to hear no evil, see no evil, speak no evil, even though evil exists around them. I wish I thought that church attendance was a reliable measure of self-discipline in sex matters, but I don't. A young minister I know in a suburb of Philadelphia gained the confidence of a young people's group in his church to the point where they talked to him frankly about their sex lives. Out of this group of thirty youngsters of high school age, only five were *not* having premarital sex relations. The youth leader, an intelligent boy, said with a shrug that he and his girl friend in the Sunday School class saw nothing wrong with their relationship, that they might get married some day or they might not, but that in the meantime no one was getting hurt. And he quoted, approvingly, a statement made by a book publisher (since convicted of pornography) to the effect that: "Sexual freedom should be permitted to the fullest extent short of injury— provable injury—to another human being."

Again and again you find this word "freedom" being used to justify conduct that is basically anti-social and therefore anti-moral. How are we going to set young people straight on this? Or older people, for that matter? How are we going to make them understand that freedom from traditional restraints is *not* the same thing as freedom to do exactly as one pleases? How are we going to make them realize that if you discard external disciplines, you must substitute internal ones, that otherwise civilization begins to crumble? These are questions that scream for answers. We will not get them so long as people keep telling themselves that nothing is wrong.

I wish some of these comfortable and complacent souls could do the reading I have done. They would get a jolt. Let me set down here a few random quotations taken from current studies of the problem that have appeared in book or periodical form. Here are comments attributed to students in some of our better universities:

"Stealing food from the dorm refrigerator would be more condemned around here than fornicating on the living room couch." RADCLIFFE SENIOR.

"Most parents and deans believe that sex is an after-dark activity that takes several hours. My generation knows that any time of day is a good time and that all you need is fifteen minutes." HARVARD JUNIOR.

"If you read in a story that a girl got pregnant, you figure that she's either been fantastically sheltered, or that, subconsciously, to use a corny term, she wanted to get pregnant. Anyway, she's got to be a pretty special case." SMITH JUNIOR.

"It isn't just the boys who pressure you into bed; it's the other girls. Not that they say anything, but just by being around them I feel like some kind of nut." COLLEGE GIRL QUOTED IN *Esquire.*

"So, sure, some girls roll in the hay a little, but they get rid of their anxieties and frustrations that way." COLUMN IN THE *Daily Californian.*

"Premarital sex doesn't mean the downfall of society; at least, not the kind of society that we're going to build." OHIO STATE SENIOR.

"Sex is so casual and taken for granted—I mean, we go to dinner, we go home, get undressed like old married people, you know—and just go to bed. I mean I'm not saying I'd like to be raped on the living room floor exactly. But I would love to just sit around on the sofa and neck." HUNTER COLLEGE STUDENT.

Well, the complacent ones may say, college kids always like to shock their elders, and their bark is much worse than their bite. All right; let's add a couple of quotations from reporters who have checked into the situation.

"On the campus where a diaphragm is a status symbol, the highest status rating goes to the girl who got her mother to foot the gynecologist's bill." GAEL GREENE, *Sex and the College Girl.*

Again, from Miss Greene: "Parents and educators will never bridge the chasm between generations until they have the courage to admit that there can be good sex outside of marriage."

"By 1975, regular copulation will be normal and expected during the engagement period. By that time, virtually no girl will graduate from college a virgin. Many, if not most, will have carried on at least one lengthy affair." JAMES L. COLLIER IN *Cavalier*.

Certainly sociologists do not dissent from these lurid evaluations. According to *Time* Magazine, Dr. Graham B. Blaine, Jr., psychiatrist to the Harvard and Radcliffe Health Service, estimates that "within the past fifteen years, the number of college boys who had intercourse before graduation rose from 50 percent to 60 percent and the number of college girls from 25 percent to 40 percent."

According to the same magazine, a Purdue sociologist estimates that one out of six brides is pregnant.

Here is *Newsweek* reporting: "Undoubtedly the key to the new morality is the widespread belief that a boy and girl who have established what the college calls a meaningful relationship have the moral right to sleep together."

This view is supported by endless surveys on endless campuses. One such survey at a famous woman's college indicated that "92 percent of those questioned approved of sex relations if the couple felt they were in love but didn't wind up as husband and wife." At Columbia, a poll of the senior class showed 83 percent of the class in favor of premarital relations, 13 percent opposed, 4 percent undecided. And so it goes.

These attitudes are not limited to college students; they are prevalent today in all age groups under fifty. Here is a lady editor describing the standards of her readers: "Anything that goes on in private between two consenting adults is moral. What is shocking now is only real promiscuity or homosexuality or sex in which more than two people participate, and even then no one would dream of interfering unless someone is forced."

Again and again, amid all the confusion and clamoring voices, you hear the plaintive question, "What difference does it make if no one is getting hurt?" This sounds fine in theory, but multiply this attitude by millions of eager experimenters and what do you get? You get such statistics as these: "Between the years 1940 and 1957 the illegitimacy rate increased 112 percent in the 15–19 age group, 300 percent in the 20–24 age group, 462 percent in the 25–29 age group, 478 percent in the 30–34 age group, 456 percent in the 35–39 age group, and 196 percent in the 40–44 age group."

More statistics? "Venereal disease among adolescents rose 10 percent between the years 1956 and 1961. Between 1955 and 1959, venereal disease rose 318 percent in New Orleans, 591 percent in San Francisco, 378 percent in Houston, 291 percent in Los Angeles, 280 percent in Washington, D.C. The illegitimacy rate has tripled since 1953. By 1970, ten million Americans will have been born out of wedlock. Forty percent of the unwed mothers are between the ages of 15 and 19."

No one is getting hurt? What a laugh! What a hollow, tragic, gruesome laugh!

And the hurt is not confined to individuals; it damages and degrades our nation throughout the world. The bitter truth is that the Communist world, the world we scorn as atheistic and cynical and immoral and dangerous, has higher standards in this area of sex behavior than we do. Sex immorality is not tolerated in the Soviet Union to anything like the extent that is accepted or even publicized here. Their theater is not preoccupied with sex abnormalities or deviation. Their literature is not riddled with eroticism. And if the Communists believe, as they obviously do, that sex obsession is a sign of degeneracy in an individual or in a nation, will they not do all in their power to foster such a trend in the nations of the West? Will they not encourage pornography and licentiousness? Will they not ridicule and deride any attempts to uphold standards of decency? Will they not remind the rest of the world at every opportunity that Americans are sex-mad and dollar-mad and unfit to be the leaders of humanity or the champions of freedom? Of course they will!

Meanwhile, we play right into their hands, by making dirtier and dirtier movies, by publishing filthier and filthier books. When Khrushchev visited Hollywood, what did we show him as a sample of American movie-making? A saga of how our pioneer ancestors won the West? A story of American medicine's great contribution to mankind? No, what we showed him was a line of half-naked chorus girls dancing the cancan, a spectacle so cheap and degrading that onlookers winced. Later, in San Francisco, the Russian leader referred to it with scorn and contempt as typical of

American culture, and even danced an obscene parody of it himself.

This sort of thing, especially when it is deliberately exported, blackens our image with the rest of the world. Mal Whitfield, our great Negro Olympic champion who worked for years for our State Department in Africa, has been quoted as saying: "The sex-mad Americans are ruining us in Africa. The impurity in the Americans is in direct proportion to the United States policy not working in Africa today."

A traveler returning from a South American capital recently reported that in the theater district one of our seamier Broadway productions was playing, while across the street a ballet company from the Soviet Union was attracting larger crowds and far more favorable attention from the critics. And a native of the city said to the traveler, "You send us plays like these; your government sponsors them. Then you ask us to support your way of life, which presumably this play depicts. You must think we're crazy!" And he added: "A house built on sand will not last; neither will a civilization built on dirt."

There is a grim, ancestral wisdom in those words. From the beginning of recorded history, men have known that the sex drive had to be controlled if civilization was to replace anarchy. From the beginning, peoples and prophets alike shared the belief that sooner or later unchecked sexual license brought down the wrath of the gods in the form of decadence, decay, and loss of creativity. Modern research substantiates this belief. Arnold Toynbee, one of the world's great historians, writes: "Of twenty-one notable civilizations, nineteen perished, not from conquest from without, but from decay within." Another historian, Dr. J. D. Unwin of Cambridge University, made a study of eighty civilizations ranging over a period of four thousand years and concluded that a society either chooses sexual promiscuity and decline, or sexual discipline and creative energy. Writes Dr. Unwin: "Any human society is free to choose either to display great energy, or to enjoy sexual freedom; the evidence is that they cannot do both for more than one generation."

What has caused us to drift away in so short a time from these time-tested guidelines? Different people offer different reasons. Perhaps we should take time to consider some of these reasons, since it is hard to cure any malady unless you know the cause. Some of these theories may seem a bit farfetched. But let's consider them anyway: the more candles we can light in the darkness, the better.

Some sociologists blame the sex revolution on the mobility and consequent instability of modern society. Not long ago I read in some historical study that in rural England, just a couple of hundred years ago, the average person never traveled more than seven miles from his home in all of his life—and came into contact with less than three hundred people! Imagine how rigidly his life was controlled by custom, by habit, by the village church, by the local squire who was also justice of the peace. Those people were born, lived, and died according to rules and regulations handed down from antiquity and sanctioned by immemorial custom.

But today people no longer stay put. They move from town to town, from job to job. This means there is less pressure to conform to accepted standards of conduct. It also means that there is less emotional security and more loneliness. Youngsters try to overcome this loneliness by going steady. Adults try to bridge the chasm with sex, legitimate or otherwise.

In addition, some psychologists feel that fear of atomic warfare is a factor, creating a "Let's-live-for-the-moment" attitude among people; or even, on a deeper level, stimulating the instinct to reproduce, to create life because life itself is threatened by extinction.

Another environmental factor may well be the sharp rise in the number of women who work. It is probably no accident that as the number of working mothers has increased, so has the incidence of juvenile delinquency of all kinds and the decline of sex morals among young people.

Yet another cause, inside the family, may be the permissiveness that has clouded our child-raising theories and practices for the past twenty or thirty years. Too many parents seem actually afraid of their children. They make little or no effort to enforce discipline. They seem to act on the helpless assumption that children can't really be controlled, so why bother to try? The result is that the children never learn discipline or how to control themselves.

Still another reason offered by students of the problem is the demand on the part of women for equality with men in all areas, including sex. I must say, I am all for equality between the sexes, and I cannot see—ethically—why the old double standard of sex conduct was ever justified. But what has happened is that, in wiping out the double standard, the women have not attempted to raise the men to their own former levels of self-respect and self-control; they have descended to the male level of promiscuity.

All these explanations may have some validity, but I think myself that there are four primary influences at work that have drastically changed and are still changing our sex attitudes.

The first is the almost incredible commercialization of sex that has taken place in the last ten or fifteen years.

The second is the virtual disappearance of two great deterrents to extramarital sex, fear of unwanted pregnancy and fear of venereal disease.

The third is what might be called the treason of some of our intellectuals—writers, thinkers, philosophers—who have done their best to make sex immorality seem natural and normal, and self-control in sex Puritanical, old-fashioned, or downright queer.

The fourth—although I hesitate to use so strong a word —is the surrender of too many of the clergy to the notion that if people fail to live up to absolute standards of morality, there must be something wrong with such standards, and that they had better be stretched or altered until fallible human beings feel more comfortable with them.

Let's consider the impact of these four influences one by one.

The urge to make money out of raw sex has reached fantastic proportions in this country. It constantly assaults the eye, the ear, and the brain. A former President of the Protestant Council of the City of New York, Arthur Lee Kinsolving, says: "The American sex drive may be constant from one generation to another, but the drive to exploit sex, to prostitute it, has become a horrendous thing in America."

Day and night the merchants of sex work on an almost defenseless public. Their cynical conviction that "sex sells" leers from every movie marquee, every newsstand, every bookstall. And it's not just sex itself that they're selling; sex is used constantly to stimulate the sale of ordinary consumer goods. Does Madison Avenue want to sell a new hair tonic for men? The pitch is no longer simply that it will keep your hair neat or wellgroomed. The pitch now is that it will drive women mad with desire for any man who uses it. Does a cosmetic company want to promote a new perfume? Any name will do, so long as it's erotic.

Does Hollywood want to fill its movie theaters with impressionable adolescents? Sexy ads in the newspapers will do it. Today Hollywood not only makes its newspaper ads as suggestive as possible, it is also growing aware that everything —even sex—has its saturation point. So now plain old adultery, infidelity, and fornication will no longer do—there must be hints of sadism, masochism, and perversions as well.

As for books, items that used to be printed only in Latin in medical volumes may be found in Anglo-Saxon English in any drugstore. Nudity is so common in magazines that publishers are beginning to ask plaintively, "What do we show after we've shown it all?"

With this barrage of sexuality emanating from every medium of communication, it is easy to see how people— especially young people—become sex-oriented and sex-obsessed. Even if they are not consciously overstimulated physically, something in them is conditioned to give sex too much attention, too much prominence in their lives. As David Riesman, a Harvard sociologist says, "There is an illusion abroad in the land that sex is the most important thing in life, and that life can be built on sex alone." Standards become subtly warped; values change. The yardstick by which achievement is measured becomes a sexual yardstick. The individual becomes caught, as one psychoanalyst has put it, in a "competitive compulsion to prove oneself an acceptable sexual machine."

What is the answer to this? I doubt if it lies in the realm of censorship; the process of liberalization has gone too far. I think and hope that the answer will lie, ultimately, in a massive revulsion against the crudity and vulgarity and sickening bad taste of the current commercialization of sex, a revulsion that will send the pendulum swinging back as it swung back after the excesses and debaucheries of Restoration England.

We probably can't make this happen tomorrow. But we can hasten the day by doing everything in our power to increase the fastidiousness and lift the standards and encourage the self-discipline of people, especially our young people. The sex peddlers can succeed only so long as there are avid and immature customers for their wares. If we can educate people to the point where they reject such trash because they know it is degrading and because it is offensive to them, then per-haps—slowly—the battle will be won and the filth peddlers, finding their incomes vanishing, will fold their verminous tents and steal away.

The second great impetus behind our changing sex morals comes from the march of science, and the impact is felt in two main areas. One is the success that medicine has had in controlling venereal disease. The other is the steady improve-ment in contraceptive devices, culminating in the market-ing of an anti-pregnancy pill that is apparently foolproof when taken under the prescribed conditions.

Fear of venereal disease as a consequence of extramarital sex has virtually disappeared from our society. This was not the case in my own youth. V.D. was much dreaded, and this fear was enhanced by sex lectures, sponsored by our college authorities, that graphically depicted the ravages of syphilis and gonorrhea. No doubt modern youngsters would smile indulgently at such a presentation, but judging from medical statistics their blithe assurance is not justified. V.D. is still around and still a menace. The V.D. rate is rising, not falling. Doctors are concerned because the wonder drugs seem to be losing some of their effectiveness. They also point out that as use of "the pill" increases, the V.D. rate may rise higher still. Some mechanical contraceptive devices offer a degree of protection against infection. The pill does not.

No one, I think, should condemn the pill itself. Some day it may prove the answer to the population explosion that threatens to overwhelm the resources of the planet. But there's little doubt that its availability is encouraging an undeter-mined number of people to experiment with sex outside of marriage. And despite its alleged effectiveness, the number of unwanted pregnancies keeps on rising.

Some psychologists offer an interesting reason for this. They say that very often the maternal instinct in women is so strong that an unconscious drive causes them to neglect precautions in order to become pregnant. Not long ago an almost distracted woman came to consult our counselors at the American Foundation of Religion and Psychiatry. She was a widow, without much money. Her son, a college junior, had been "going steady" with a girl. The girl had become pregnant. The woman told us tearfully that her son was de-termined to marry the girl and give the baby a name. But, she added, if he did this he would have to cut short his education, go to work, give up his plans to go to medical school. The mother was heartbroken. Naturally, she laid most of the blame on the girl. It was easy to see that she hoped her son would ignore his responsibilities in the matter, abandon the girl, proceed with his education, and become the neurosurgeon his mother had always hoped he would be.

But the boy had no such intention. (Our records show that quite a high percentage of the boys involved in premarital affairs, perhaps because of a latent sense of guilt, are prepared to marry the girl "if anything goes wrong.") He told us that he was ready to take up the first job he could get. "My girl told me," he said, "that she was taking the pill. But I guess it doesn't work, or something. Anyway, we're trapped. There's no other solution that I can see."

We also talked to the girl. She said that she had no difficulty in obtaining the pill without a doctor's prescription. But she finally admitted that she had not followed directions when it came to taking it. To suppress ovulation, the pill must be taken for twenty days consecutively each month. "I tried to remember," she said. "But sometimes I'd forget. I'd take one every day for a few days. Then I'd go for a while without taking any. I must have been out of my mind."

Actually, she wasn't out of her mind at all; it was her deeper mind that was making her forget to take the pill. One of our psychiatrists said to me: "This is a clear-cut case where 'being in love,' used as an excuse for premarital sex relations, leads to pregnancy. Very often, when a woman is in love, she not only wants to bind the man to her in every possible way, she also wants instinctively to bear his child. This urge, this life-force, can be so strong that it simply pushes reason aside and takes charge of the situation. This is one of those cases, and there must be tens of thousands of others." He added: "If I were a young man trying to avoid matrimony, I'd write six words on a piece of paper and paste them on my bathroom mirror where I'd see them every morning. Those six words would be, 'Beware of the power of love!' "

But that boy had no one to give him such a warning, and now will never be the surgeon he had hoped to be.

The third main reason for the drastic upheaval in our sex habits and attitudes is the influence of some of our intellectuals. Sharp changes in customs or attitudes do not begin at the bottom of a society, they start at the top. Ideas don't rise up; they filter down. Sooner or later a civilization tends to become what its thinkers have been thinking.

And what have our most vocal thinkers been thinking? In too many cases they have been thinking and writing and preaching—not just liberalism in sex, but freedom from all authority, freedom from all restraints.

This trend began some fifty years ago as a revolt against Victorian prudery, and no one denies today that Victorian attitudes toward sex were rigid, repressive, and unrealistic. But the curious thing was that the revolt was led, more often than not, by individuals whose attitudes toward sex were hardly normal in the first place. Dean Fitch has pointed this out in an article in the *Christian Century*. Speaking of the vanguard of this revolt against prudery, he had this to say about the leaders: "Schopenhauer clearly hated sex. Shaw, like Schopenhauer, linked sex with life-force, but by deliberate contract refrained from it in his own marriage. Freud was quite decorous in his own conduct and had a mild sex drive that terminated early in life. Havelock Ellis, with all his sex mysticism, was sexually impotent for the better part of his career. And Walt Whitman, who touted sex so brazenly in verse, almost certainly never knew a woman in the flesh."

Gradually—and perhaps inevitably—the revolt against repressiveness in sex became a revolt against conventional morals. It was Hemingway, idol of a whole generation, who could write that: "What is moral is what you feel good after and what is immoral is what you feel bad after." What nonsense! Under this weird code of ethics Hitler could have told himself that slaughtering the Jews was a moral act because it made him feel happy. And a man as intelligent as Hemingway must have known this. But millions of impressionable people gladly accepted this dictum as some kind of moral gospel.

Again, take a modern writer like Helen Gurley Brown, who wrote a best seller called *Sex and the Single Girl*. Mrs. Brown is a first-rate writer, crisp, intelligent, amusing. But her book is one long glorification of indiscriminate sex. If a girl who happens to be a virgin reads it uncritically, she will almost certainly put it down wondering how on earth she can be so backward, unenlightened, convention-ridden, and stupid. Sex, according to Mrs. Brown, is fun, so why not try it? The penalties suffered by many of those who follow her advice do not seem to concern her.

It is probably unfair to single out Mrs. Brown's book as a symbol of social irresponsibility where sex is concerned. because this attitude has dominated our popular literature and our theaters for several decades now. Best-selling novels usually chronicle endless sexual exploits that are laughable to anyone who has the faintest understanding of human nature or human biology. But such books easily may —and doubtless do—lead impressionable people to wonder what is wrong with them since their own sex lives fall so far short of these lurid fantasies.

Individually, perhaps, these books are not very influential. But cumulatively they are. And sometimes, when talent and cynicism team up, the impact on vast audiences becomes enormous. If you ever want to make a study in contrasts, I suggest you compare the thrillers of the late John Buchan, who almost two generations ago wrote *The Thirty-nine Steps*, as well as other spy stories, with those of the late Jan Fleming, whose hero, James Bond, is currently the idol of countless armchair adventurers and moviegoers. There is violence in Buchan's books, true, but no sadism, and no exploitative sex at all. Fleming's books are saturated with both.

An historian might well point out that similar trends in entertainment standards took place in ancient Rome. There the spectacles in the Colosseum, which began with gladiators fighting one another, or wild animals fighting other animals gradually degenerated—under pressure from the crowds for newer and more special "kicks"—to torture and sadism and finally sex orgies and perversions. It's a little frightening to contemplate this parallel and ask yourself at what point on the long slide our own civilization now stands. It becomes even more terrifying when you remind yourself that the sands of time run faster now than they did then, and that changes that once took decades or even centuries now seem to come about in mere years.

I don't think our standards would ever have fallen so low if some really first-class minds hadn't provided the initial push. Now and then, in a flash of honesty, the intellectuals themselves will admit this. Peter Howard, an Oxford graduate and formerly a top-flight reporter for the Beaverbrook press in London, was the leader of the Moral Re-Armament movement until his recent, untimely death. Here is what he

said in a speech given at Williams College about his own role
and that of another famous intellectual in England:

"My generation at Oxford had a funny outlook. Aldous
Huxley was one of our great heroes. We were absolutely
determined that no one should tell us what to do. But we
used our brains to tell our conscience and our heart that
what we wanted was right. We succeeded.

"And then some of us did something even more far-
reaching. We got important jobs and used our Oxford-
trained intelligence to kill the conscience of the nation in
order to make the nation more comfortable for us to live
in. I think that was pretty good dictatorship. But of course
we did it in the name of liberty.

"Then Huxley grew older. This is what he said some years
later in *Ends and Means*:

'I had motives for not wanting the world to have a meaning,
consequently assumed it had none, and was able without difficulty to find satisfying reasons for this assumption. For myself,
as no doubt for most of my contemporaries, the philosophy
of meaninglessness was essentially a matter of liberation. The
liberation we desired was simultaneously a liberation from a
certain kind of political and economic system and liberation
from a certain system of morality. We objected to the morality because it interfered with our sexual freedom.'

"That," Peter Howard added, "is a very honest statement."
Well, so it is, and I admire Huxley for making it. But
where were the traditional guardians of morals when the
intellectuals attacked them? Where, to put it bluntly, was the
church? This brings me to the fourth great underlying cause
of the sex revolution—the increasing hesitancy and uncertainty of the Protestant church where sex morals are concerned.

"The church," writes Charles Malik, the brilliant Christian
scholar from Lebanon, "has always been the keeper of men's
consciences, the guardian of morals. If the people grow
selfish or materialistic or lazy, it is the duty of the church
to point an accusing finger, to insist on drastic and immediate
change. This the church has *not* been doing, not with the
indignation and eloquence and authority that are needed."

It certainly hasn't. In fact, it seems to me that some of
the leaders of the church are guilty of encouraging the sex

revolution by obliquely or openly advocating drastic change
in moral standards.

These men probably mean well. They like to point ou
that Christ was opposed to many of the religious laws and
taboos of His time; which He was. They add that He deal
with individuals according to the circumstances in which H
found them, not according to rigid rules. This is also true
But when they go on to argue that special circumstances ca
therefore sometimes justify departures from accepted mora
teachings, then they are in trouble. They are in trouble be
cause, once you begin to qualify your absolutes, even slightly
it becomes almost impossible to stop, and if the process goe
very far, you find the bedrock of moral certainty beginning
to crumble under your feet.

When I was a child, for instance, preachers in rural Ohic
used to preach against smoking, drinking, and any kind of
sexual activity outside of marriage. Then the ban against
smoking was modified so that it applied only to women.
Finally smoking became widely accepted—no one argued
against it any more. Next, in some denominations, the bans
against drinking went down. Soon it became accepted practice for ministers to take a drink, or several. Now we have
an occasional far-out clergyman who accommodates to down-
graded moral standards by seeming to imply that premarital
sex relations are maybe not too bad after all if the couple
eventually marry. Perhaps before long even this qualification
may disappear.

My point is, where do you draw the line? The danger,
once you've abandoned your absolute, is that you will keep
on drawing temporary lines and then stepping over them,
until there are no standards left.

Let me make one other rather depressing point. I think
much of the pressure on ministers to water down rules and
lower standards come from other ministers. No one likes to
feel old-fashioned, or behind the times. But that's what you're
made to feel nowadays if you try to hold the line where
morals are concerned. I still preach against premarital or
extramarital sex from my pulpit for reasons which I hope
to spell out in the next chapter. But I'll admit that sometimes, when I do so, I wonder if younger or more liberal
ministers who hear or read my sermons may not be smiling
indulgently, or writing me off as some kind of antiquated
mossback. The bleak truth is, most of us would rather be

considered almost anything than naïve. But if you're a conservative in this area of sex morals, that's what you're made to feel by some of your colleagues today. The result, I'm convinced, is that many ministers are shying away from taking a stand. They prefer to remain on the sidelines. They don't actually condone what they think is immoral, but they don't condemn it either, and their silence hangs like a pall over the church.

Unfortunate though it is, this silence is probably less damaging in the long run than the influence of some ministers ho argue, in effect, that the moral code should be revised until it conforms to prevailing practices. "Times change," these reformists cry; "customs change. People are more knowledgeable today, more sophisticated than they were. You can't expect them to live under the same rules as the Puritans or the Victorians."

Well, it's true that times change, and so do customs. But —and here is where it seems to me the reformists go off the track—basic moral principles don't change. If adultery was wrong in the days of the Puritans, it is wrong still. If fornication was wrong in Christ's time—and He said it was —it isn't right today. Man-made conventions may change. The Victorian system of chaperonage, for instance, has gone with the wind; and maybe it *was* too restrictive, too authoritarian, too suspicious of human nature. But its disappearance doesn't make today's promiscuity a good or healthy state of affairs.

This distinction between eternal ethical laws and shifting patterns of social behavior is not being made clearly and forcibly by the people whose job it is to make it, namely, the leaders of the church. They are leaving the teaching of morals to laymen—sociologists, psychologists, medicine men of all kinds. And the result, not very surprisingly, is a kind of ethical chaos.

Even laymen, sometimes, grow concerned over this tendency of the church to adopt a permissive or relativistic approach to morals. Here's a bit of viewing-with-alarm that I encountered recently. "There is a vast difference between recognizing human frailty and lending it the seeming sanction of authority. The wisdom of the decalogue is not repealed because some people commit adultery." Is this distant thunder from some indignant pulpit or church periodical? No, it's from the *Wall Street Journal*. And the

Journal is right: too often the ideas held by church intellectuals *do* seem to lend sanction to conduct that our grandfathers would have unhesitatingly labeled immoral.

Last summer in London an Anglican theologian with whom I discussed the problem shrugged his shoulders. "The moral code that we've been teaching has to be revised," he said. "It simply doesn't work any more. Not 2 percent of the people in our church believe in it or live by it. What good i a moral code if no one lives up to it?" He went on to discuss sex at great length in terms of "meaningful relationships." These relationships, he said, should not be based on moral laws, but on concern for other people. Sex, he added, was the means whereby one person could reach another at the deepest level and at the same time discover new things about himself. That was what we should try to get across to our congregations, especially the younger members.

I must say, my reaction to this was a fervent wish that middle-aged Anglican theologians would stay in their cloistered halls and debate learned topics among themselves, not attempt to guide young people through the crises and temptations that they are likely to encounter in the back seat of a parked car. They mean well, but too often their fine-spun theories are misunderstood and misapplied and twisted into justification for conduct that is surely the last thing they meant to advocate. And then somebody else has to pick up the pieces!

What these Protestant theorists don't seem to understand (I think most Roman Catholic priests do) is that an adolescent becomes sexually mature long before he is emotionally mature. You aren't going to make any real impression on such a person with nice distinctions as to the ultimate purpose and meaning of sex. You just have to hammer home hard-bitten reasons why the sex drive has to be controlled, and do it in the plainest and most compelling way you can.

Perhaps I will be accused of anti-intellectualism, and of thinking with my heart instead of my head, but every instinct and every bit of counseling experience I have had tells me that sex is too explosive and dangerous a commodity to be handed over to immature people with no strings attached. It's too much like letting a small child decide for himself whether or not to run across a traffic-filled intersection. He just doesn't have the judgment. You can explain the hazards to him, you can point out the dangers, but then you have to say "Don't!" and make it stick.

This belief of mine does not contradict the theme of this book, which is the need for self-responsibility. It simply recognizes that a process of growth is required before self-responsibility becomes possible, and that until that growth is achieved, people must be protected—even against themselves. Otherwise they may damage or even destroy themselvs before they get within shouting distance of true self-control.

I think the time has come for the church to shake off its bemused and sometimes fuzzy-minded preoccupation with "love-controlled interpersonal relationships" and once more hold up absolute standards of honesty and unselfishness and personal decency for people to measure themselves by. Of course people are going to fall short of the absolutes; they always did and they always will. But the truth is, if you are to have a standard, it must be absolute; otherwise it is no standard at all. This really is what Christianity has to offer. It offers a standard in the life and person of Christ Himself. Christ was sent to teach us how to live, and He showed us how in His own amazing and magnificent life.

It's ironic—and a little frightening—to think that where this whole confused, cloudy, complicated business of morals is concerned, some of us have the answer, have had it all along, but lack the faith and the eloquence and the power to put it across. I'm talking about the clergy—myself included.

Wouldn't it be wonderful if we ministers could put aside all fine-spun abstraction, if we could stop offering complicated theories of behavior to people, if we could forget about rigid rules and regulations and simply say to anyone who would hear us: "Look, we know you yearn for happiness and fulfillment. We know you are groping for an answer to the confusion and pain and puzzlement of living. Well, there *is* an answer, and you can have it. Not by loading yourself with restrictions and prohibitions. Not by running away from responsibilities or giving in to weakness. But simply by accepting a Person in your life, by opening a door and admitting a Personality so strong and vital and radiant that you are irresistibly attracted to Him, and want to obey and follow Him.

"That Person is Christ, and when you take Him into your life, really accept Him as friend and guide and the perfect model for living, then problems of moral behavior fade into the background. You don't have to struggle to do the right thing. You do it instinctively, and the closer you are to Christ, the more effortless right-thinking and right-acting become. You no longer have to search and grope for moral yardsticks. All you have to do is ask yourself if Christ would approve of what you are doing, and let your conscience answer. If you know Christ, and if you follow the voice of your conscience, you'll never go wrong."

Yes, it would be wonderful if we ministers could say that, and if people listened and acted accordingly. Obviously we have a long, long way to go. It's almost as if the answer were too simple, too good to be true, too wonderful to be believed. So poeple keep on looking for other answers.

Of course there are other answers, answers that you can give people who cannot or will not accept the best and final answer.

Let's take a look at some of them in the next chapter.

CHAPTER V

Sin, Sex and Self-Control

"To preach morality is easy," wrote Schopenhauer; "to find a foundation for morality is hard." Now, there's a somber statement for you! Of course, Schopenhauer was a pretty gloomy fellow. He was a famous philosopher, but he was also a negative thinker, poor chap.

Actually, I don't think it's very hard to find a foundation for morality. If you deal as much with people as I do, you become convinced not through some high-flown theory, but from plain, everyday observation—that life is so arranged that morality and happiness go hand in hand. Conversely, immoral behavior makes people miserable. Not right away in some cases, perhaps. And perhaps never in the rare instance when a person has been able to kill his conscience completely. But by and large, sooner or later, day in day out, immoral conduct is a sterile, disheartening, destructive business.

This is probably more true in the area of sex ethics than anywhere else. You may cheat on your income tax and rationalize it fairly successfully. You may try to persuade a traffic policeman not to give you a summons by slipping a ten-dollar bill with your driver's license. This sort of behavior erodes your standards and diminishes you as a person, of course. But it doesn't rock the foundations of your soul the way tampering with the sex code does. When you begin bending the ancient moral laws of sexual behavior, it's a little like experimenting with the heart of the atom. You can unlock forces that will destroy you.

I'll agree with Schopenhauer to this extent: it's hard to make people believe in the value of morality until they get their fingers burned. In fact there are times, preaching in my pulpit, when I wonder if it wouldn't be more effective to use tape recordings, concealing identities of course, of some of the conversations I have had in the privacy of my office with men and women who have been caught in the whirlwinds of sex and are trying somehow to regain their equilibrium and restore their damaged lives. Such tape recordings, played on Sunday morning from the pulpit, might have more impact and might do more good than anything I could say in my role as minister.

No two stories, of course, are alike. And no two people are alike. Some are guilt-ridden, some are not. Some are remorseful, some defiant. But through all these tangled tales of premarital or extramarital sex adventures runs a somber thread of disillusionment, a kind of weary realization that the whole thing wasn't worth it, emotionally or any other way. And there, I think, is the answer—the harsh, blunt, pragmatic answer—to Mr. Schopenhauer. The ultimate foundation for morality is that immorality doesn't work, it doesn't pay off. It doesn't lighten the burden of living. It increases it.

Only last week I found myself talking to a woman, intelligent, sensitive, sophisticated. She said frankly that she had come to see me because she needed an escape valve. "I'm not very religious," she said. "I just need to talk about this thing. It's sitting at the pit of my stomach like one of those pronged anchors we used to use with our sailboat. I know enough about psychiatry to understand the need for and value of 'ventilation.' So here I am, probably wasting your time."

"You're not wasting it," I said. "That's what I'm here for."

So she told me about her love affair.

I believe some one once defined immorality as acute short-sightedness. I always think of this when I find myself trying to deal with people who have become involved in extramarital affairs. When they fall into them, they never seem to look ahead; they're too caught up with what seems to be the excitement and daring and romance of the moment. They never stop to think about the basic discontents that are pushing them, either, or what might be done to set them right. They just plunge in.

As is so often the case, this woman's infidelity seemed to be based on her resentment of shortcomings, real or fancied, in her husband. "Somehow," she said, "by destroying his exclusive right to me as a woman, I seemed to be paying him back for his drinking and his indifference and his hypochon-

dria and so on. Well, I paid him back, all right. I paid quite
a price myself. To begin with, I got far more involved with
my lover emotionally than he was with me. Do you realize
how humiliating this can be to a woman? To find yourself
living in terror because a man who doesn't belong to you
anyway may slam the door on you? Which of course is what
happened, in the end, in spite of all my tears and pleadings
and grovelings. God, it makes me cringe to look back on it!"

I noticed that she was twisting a handkerchief between her
fingers. I wondered how the little piece of linen could stand
the strain.

"I don't think a woman can ever really strike a balance in
a clandestine love affair," she said. "Not if she has any
sensitivity or fastidiousness at all. Either you don't really
care about the man, and get disgusted with yourself and the
whole thing. Or else you care too much, and drive yourself
crazy wanting more of him than you can ever have. Then
there are all sorts of dandy little dividends that you never
hear your sophisticates talk about. Going in at night and
looking at your children asleep in bed and knowing that one
false step on the tightrope—just one—and you could warp
and damage their lives forever. Going to dinner at your
parents' home, and feeling their love and pride surround
you, and wondering what would happen to that love and
pride if they knew. Seeing your lover at a party and feeling
your heart turn over—and then watching your husband greet
him with trust and friendliness. Oh, it's great, just great, believe me!"

"I believe you," I said.

"And the knowledge, building up in you all the time no
matter how you try to suppress it, that something in you is
being washed away, some kind of self-esteem that is essential
to happiness. And the awareness, although you try to ignore
it, that by diverting all this energy and time and loyalty
you're weakening your capacity to meet your obligations
in the fundamental areas of life: marriage, and child-rearing,
and . . . and . . . Damn it, I swore I wouldn't cry and here
I am crying."

"Go ahead," I said. "Something in you needs to."

She made a little hopeless gesture. "I'm not crying just
for myself," she said. "I'm crying for people, and the world,
and all the pitiful broken dreams, and the desperate, selfish

clutching at happiness, and the way life runs over us and tramples us all."

"You're emotionally exhausted," I told her. "You've put yourself through a wringer. You went on a spiritual binge and now you're suffering a spiritual hangover. That's one more penalty of breaking these old time-tested laws. Why do you think we have them? Precisely to spare people the kind of suffering you're going through! But I think that if you see your mistakes, as you do, and are sorry for them, as you are, and don't repeat them, as you probably won't, you'll find forgiveness."

"I don't know about that," she said sadly; "I did what I did, didn't I?"

"Every day," I told her, "is an opportunity not to repeat a mistake; every day is an opportunity to do better. That's a form of forgiveness, isn't it?"

She smiled a little. "I suppose so," she said. And so she went away, leaving me to wish that others could have heard what she said and learned by example to avoid a situation so full of hidden heartache. It would be so much less painful and damaging than learning it, as she did, the hard way.

Here, you see, was another case where the old rules were ignored or set aside but there were no inner controls to take their place. If this woman had set her "obligations in the fundamental areas of life" squarely in front of her and lived up to them, perhaps she wouldn't have needed the old rules. But she failed to do this. She tried to live without the rule book. And she got hurt.

I find it difficult, speaking only for myself now, to judge such persons too harshly. They have fallen into a trap, it's true; they have been willful and disobedient if you like. But the trap is baited with the cleverest and deadliest of lures: ego starvation plus sex attraction. No wonder our ancestors used to equate these sex transgressions with the workings of the Devil. To the hapless victim, the opportunities for wrongdoing are made to look so attractive, so desirable, at times even so apparently justifiable, that it's not too farfetched to see behind them a mighty and sinister Intelligence, a principle of evil, active and malevolent, consciously working against the principle of Good. I know that the concept of the Devil at work seems quaint and old-fashioned and remote in these sophisticated times. But I'm not sure that the idea would seem so fantastic to the woman who wept in my office last week.

I must confess that there are times, especially after a difficult counseling session, when I can't help comparing my role as a minister with that of my clergyman father. And in a way I envy him, because his task was a good deal simpler. By and large, in these sex tangles, he was dealing with people for whom sin was a vivid reality, and I'm pretty sure that when a member of his flock strayed from the straight and narrow path he didn't have to persuade or reason or cajole. He could tell the transgressor flatly that sex outside of marriage was contrary to the will of God, and cite chapter and verse from the Bible to support his statement. In those days, if the sinner believed in God and accepted the promise that the Bible was divine revelation, then he had no answer except the rather terrifying one that he chose deliberately to go on disobeying and defying God. And not many people were willing to take such a stand.

I believe, myself, that the Bible *is* the word of God and that eternal wisdom shines through its pages. But I also know that its authority has been drastically weakened in my lifetime. There are various reasons for this. Perhaps the chief one is our generation's worship of science, with its emphasis on laboratory experimentation and verifiable proof. In any case, when the modern minister attempts to deal with the sex revolution, he can no longer simply throw the book at people, not even the Good Book. More often than not he finds himself dealing with men and women to whom God is a remote abstraction, to whom the Bible is a quaint mixture of history and legend, and to whom man-made rules, being man-made, are fallible and variable and anything but absolute.

So the modern minister has a more complex problem. Or rather, he must work out more complex solutions. The problem, actually, is the same as it has always been, and the responsibility of the minister is the same, too. It is to make people see, and agree, that where sex is concerned, self-discipline is better for them, more intelligent, more honest, more rewarding than laxity. It is the minister's job to get across the idea that the Christian demand for personal purity is not based *solely* on divine law as revealed in the Scriptures. It is also an argument based on results. It is the insistence, buttressed by twenty centuries of human experience, that the rewards of sexual control are worth having and that the penalties of sexual license sooner or later are grim, painful, destructive, and negative.

Only when we convince people, both rationally and emotionally, of these things; only when we supply clear evidence that in casual sex the game is not worth the candle, will we be able to reverse the trend toward anarchy in this, the most intimate of all relationships.

How do we do it? Not, I'm sure, by uttering halfhearted don'ts. A halfhearted don't is worse than no don't at all. No, you have to have a whole arsenal of arguments and persuasions and reasons for self-control in matters of sex. And you have to choose your weapons coolly and selectively: some for youngsters whose main problem is premarital sex, some for married people whose chief temptation is extramarital sex, and some for the argumentative souls of any age who are well equipped to look you in the eye and hurl searching and challenging questions at *you*.

Furthermore, it's not enough just to make people see the need for self-control and then piously urge them to have it. You have to offer them specific techniques for acquiring such controls. Otherwise all your arguments and persuasions will be wasted.

Let's assume for a moment that you are the parent of a boy who's a high school junior or a girl who is about to begin her freshman year at college. Let's further suppose—a big assumption, I'll admit—that you could discuss this matter of sex with them freely and without embarrassment. What should your approach be? What should you say? What sort of attitudes should you try to create in them?

I think, first of all, you should be realistic about some things. Young people are going to experiment with sex: they always have and they always will. It's silly to pretend that they won't. And up to a point, such experimentation does no harm. It's only when it passes the point of no return—the point where complete sex relations become inevitable or actual—that the parents (and society in general) have deep and valid cause for alarm.

Next, it's worth reminding yourself that youngsters are always in a state of rebellion. Each generation has to break away from the preceding generation, find itself, establish its own way of doing things and looking at things. We did this in our own youth. Our children's children will do it in theirs.

Sometimes I think it helps to tell a youngster that you are aware of his resistance to rules, and that you understand it because it's perfectly natural and all of us have our share of it. I remember once walking across the campus at a prep school with one of the schoolmasters when a youngster came running past at headlong speed. The master called out good-naturedly, "Run, Johnny, run!" Instantly Johnny stopped running and began to walk! Why? Because by disregarding the voice of authority he was scoring a little triumph that made him feel stronger and more important in his own eyes.

But when you make this admission to a youngster, you've got to carry it a step further and make him see that there is one authority that he won't resent—and that authority is himself. If *he* gives the orders, if *he* demands the discipline, if *he* sets the standards high, then he won't resent the controls.

And then I think you have got to go a step beyond that, and point out that where sex behavior is concerned, the forces involved are so powerful that unless a person is some kind of superman he will need guidelines to follow. He will need the wisdom of a moral code and the restraints that have been worked out by civilized nations over the centuries. He will need the help and guidance of religion, too.

Suppose the youngster doesn't buy this? Suppose he tells you that he has observed that moral codes vary from place to place, and from one century to another, and that the voice of religion is too negative and restrictive. Suppose he challenges the wisdom of the ages with hardboiled specific questions. What do you do then?

You meet the questions head-on, that's what you do. If you try to duck them, you are lost—you'll simply convince your challenger that there are no valid answers. The other day I was talking with a young minister who works closely with youth groups. We were discussing this business of sex morals, and he drew a piece of paper from his pocket. "I've made a list," he said, "of the four arguments I get thrown at me most often. Take a look at them. I've put the cruder ones first."

I glanced at the four items. They went like this:

1. *Sex is just another appetite like being hungry or thirsty, so why not satisfy it? Why all the fuss?*

2. *Sex is fun, or would be if we didn't let our Puritan heritage interfere and make us feel guilty. Why don't we shake off the taboos and enjoy ourselves?*

3. *Sex is a private affair. Whatever two people do in private is nobody's business.*

4. *If we love each other, what's wrong with expressing our love in this basic way?*

I handed the slip of paper back to my friend. "They all sound very familiar," I said.

"Do you have the answers?" he wanted to know.

I said that I hoped I did. He asked me to summarize them for him, because he needed all the ammunition he could get. So after he left I called in my secretary and dictated four replies, as follows:

1. *The notion that sex is just another appetite is hopelessly naïve. It may be a "natural" activity, but it differs from all other personal functions. Eating and sleeping and so on are individual actions. Sex is interpersonal—it directly affects another person. And it can have consequences that reach far beyond the two people involved. So it's not simply "like drinking a glass of water when you're thirsty."*

Anyone who wants proof of this should take a look at what happened in Russia during the early stages of the Revolution. At first there was a deliberate attempt to destroy marriage and the family. Divorces could be had for any reason at any time. Abortions were legal and easily available. Premarital relations were encouraged. Extramarital sex was decreed normal. And what happened? Listen to Professor Sorokin of Harvard University:

"Within a few years, hordes of wild, homeless children became a real menace to the Soviet Union itself. Millions of lives, especially of young girls, were wrecked; divorce skyrocketed, as did abortions. The hatreds and conflicts between polygamous and polyandrous mates rapidly mounted—and so did psycho-neuroses. Work in the nationalized factories slackened.

"The total results were so appalling that the government

was forced to reverse its policy. The propaganda of the 'glass of water' theory was declared to be counter-revolutionary, and its place was taken by official glorification of premarital chastity and of the sanctity of marriage."

In other words, the Russians found out the hard way that sex, treated as "just another appetite," will not only ruin individual lives, it will rapidly wreck the state itself.

2. *The argument that sex-is-fun-so-why-not-enjoy-it is also too limited and too simplified a view of something that is profoundly complex and fundamental. When a youngster throws this challenge at you, I think you have to say, "Look, you're only cheating one person by confining yourself to the purely physical aspects of sex. And that person is yourself. It's like buying a shiny new car with no engine! After all, you're not just an animal with purely biological needs. You're a unique, complicated individual with deep spiritual hungers and goals. Why do you respond to beauty? Why do you have a sense of justice? Why do you admire courage? These are the spiritual elements in your life. Sex also has this aspect, a non-physical side that gives it a whole new dimension. When you ignore this, you're just short-changing yourself. So get with it, boy; use your head!"*

Incidentally, this appeal to intelligence is more effective with youngsters than you might think. As Lowell Thomas pointed out in a newspaper article recently, where delinquency or poor sex standards among teen-agers are concerned, you can't make much impression by simply telling them how wrong they are. They don't mind being called immoral, that's a kind of twisted accolade. But they do mind being called stupid!

And that's what this sex-for-kicks-only approach really is. Ask any honest libertine (if you can find one!) what happens when sex is pursued for fun only, for the physical thrill and nothing more. What happens is that it becomes progressively less exciting, less thrilling, more barren, and more sterile. That's why so many of these people turn eventually to alcohol, or drugs, or twisted versions of sex, anything that seems to offer new kicks.

I read a grim commentary on this the other day in a national magazine (*Look*). It quoted a college girl as saying: "We mature at the age of twelve. We become world-weary with the boredom of the prostitute who has seen too much of life at the age of sixteen. At eighteen we are ready to die."

That might well be an epitaph for people who argue that sex is fun, so why not make the most of it.

> 3. *The argument that sex is a private affair and therefore no concern of anyone else is probably the easiest to refute. No matter how private it seems to be, extramarital sex is a threat to society as a whole, and a menace to the long-term happiness of the people involved.*

Sometimes, I'll admit, you have to hammer this through some pretty thick skulls. "What's society got to do with me?" a sullen youngster once asked me.

"Just this," I told him. "Society *is* you. It's your relationship to every person you meet, every single day. You can't get out of it any more than you can get out of your skin. Everything you do affects society. Even your thoughts affect it."

"How do you figure that?" he demanded.

"You believe in sleeping with your girl friend—right? That's an attitude, based on a thought. Now that attitude, in you and others like you, produces a quarter of a million illegitimate babies in this country every year. That affects society, doesn't it? It's responsible for Heaven knows how many abortions, forced marriages, consequent divorces. That puts quite a dent in society, doesn't it?"

"We take precautions," he said defiantly.

"Maybe you do," I said. "But they're not foolproof." I told him about the subconscious drives that sometimes lead girls to neglect precautions in order to get pregnant and that sometimes impel a boy to try to demonstrate his virility by impregnating a girl. "So the risk is there," I said. "What's more, the risk isn't confined to wrecking your own life plans, or those of your sex partner. There is also the risk of doing frightful injustice to a third person, the child who may be called into existence and whose life may be warped and twisted before it even starts. Haven't you any imagination or sense of fair play at all? Don't you believe that every child who is born has the right to be wanted and kept and loved by responsible parents? Can't you see that not only the actual conception, but even running the risk of conceiving an out-of-wedlock child is a crime?"

My sullen friend's forehead was furrowed. "I never thought much about that," he said.

Again the definition of immorality as acute shortsightedness crossed my mind. "Well, you might begin to think about it," I told him. "And even if you can't generate much concern about what your conduct may do to society, you ought to be worried about what it may do to you. Do you intend to marry this girl eventually?"

"We might get married some day," he said.

"Do you want that marriage to end in divorce?"

He shook his head slowly. "No."

"Well," I said, "you might give some thought to the figures assembled by the late Dr. Kinsey, whose report I'm sure you've heard of. Kinsey made an analysis of the connection between premarital sex and postmarital fidelity. He found that women who have had premarital sex experience are more than twice as likely to be unfaithful as those who haven't. So you might give that a little thought, too!"

These negative reasons for not indulging in premarital sex are not, perhaps, as compelling as some of the positive reasons I shall come to in a moment. But as I said earlier, the counselor needs a whole arsenal of arguments—not just a halfhearted "Don't" or a threadbare, "Well, it isn't right."

4. *The argument that anything goes if you're in love is one of the most popular among youngsters. For one thing, when a boy is trying to overcome a girl's reluctance, this approach often works. For another thing, this is the area where the traditional stand of the church is being weakened by clergymen who are saying, "Well, we've got to make some concessions or we're going to lose the ball game entirely. So* maybe *if the young people are in love, and* maybe *if they are going to be married anyway, and* maybe *if the circumstances are thus and so, then* maybe *a little interpersonal fellowship or depth relationship between them isn't so bad. Mind you, we're not saying it's good! But maybe we can recapture a*

little credit with these young people if we say it isn't so bad."

What these enlightened clerics are really saying is, "Well, if you think you're in love and want to sleep together, we'll try to understand. We'll certainly look the other way."

You don't have to be a profound student of human nature to figure out that this fuzzy approach is going to be more popular than the tough, demanding standards that have characterized Christianity in the past. The old approach was never easygoing. It said, "This sex impulse is just about the most powerful force inside you. You have got to conquer and control it, or it will conquer and control you. So stand fast!" There were no maybes, no compromises. You succeeded, or you failed. And a lot of people did fail. But at least they knew they were failing. They could see the standard, even when they didn't live up to it, and the standard never wavered.

But now, if the "progressives" in the clergy keep talking —or rather, mumbling—about maybe this and maybe that and the value of I-Thou relationships and the role of fellowship in sex, and the mysteries of mutually supportive relationships and so on, far into the night, the standards are going to become so blurred that they will have little or no meaning and morals will become both private and relative, which means that there are no morals at all.

One trouble with the we're-in-love-so-why-not? school of thought is that the great majority of human beings have a marvelous gift for sincere self-deception. Given any or no excuse at all, most of us can convince ourselves of anything we want to believe. So it's easy enough for young people to mistake passion, or an urge for conquest, or even a desire to please for love itself. And thus the word "love" becomes a kind of rubber stamp that is used to justify relationships that fall far short of love.

You can even argue, with considerable logic, that indulgence in premarital sex proves that a state of non-love exists. This is a thought, I must admit, that rarely occurs to the people involved. But sometimes it's worth pointing out to them. Once, I remember, after I had given a talk at a youth conference, a small group lingered to ask questions, and quite a lively discussion ensued. Inevitably, several of the youngsters voiced their conviction that being in love was the real criterion, the magic touchstone that converted bad behavior into good. Sex without love, they said, was bad. Sex with love was good. It was just as simple as that.

I singled out a tall, good-looking boy. "Well," I said to him, "are you in love?"

"Yes, sir," he said promptly.

"How do you know?" I asked him.

He smiled a bit self-consciously. But he stood his ground. "I know," he said, "because I've found the right girl. Even before I met her, I had an image of her in my mind. I knew what I wanted her to be like. I wanted her to be pretty, naturally. And intelligent. I wanted her to have a lot of personality. And I wanted her to love me."

"And now you've found her?"

"Yes," he said. "I have."

"Well, that's fine," I said, "as far as it goes. But let's look at your concept of what constitutes love. You say you had a kind of checklist in mind before you even met this girl. And that she measures up in all respects. Isn't that a rather narrow—even a selfish—approach to love? In each of those categories, you were really saying, 'This is what *I* want, this is what *I* must have.' Apparently you're more concerned with what you can get out of this relationship than what you can give. Is that right?"

"No sir," he said stoutly. "There's more to it than that. I care a lot about this girl. I try to give her as much as I get."

"Do you care about her welfare?" I asked him. "About her peace of mind? About her long-range happiness?"

He flushed a bit, because he saw where I was leading him. "Of course I do," he said.

"Well," I told him, "in that case I don't see how you can justify asking her or persuading her to sleep with you before you're married. You're putting her in jeopardy, in danger, in a situation where at the very least she'll have to struggle with her conscience, try to stifle it, disregard the ideals her parents have tried to implant in her, perhaps violate the moral teachings of her religion. Is this an act of love? It seems to me it's just the reverse. Real love, if you want a rough definition, is the willingness to put some one else's welfare and happiness ahead of your own desires. That's precisely what you're *not* doing. So maybe you're *not* in love." I glanced at the other youngsters. "Love always includes responsibility, remember that. If what you're feeling doesn't include it, then it isn't love. You can't have one without the other!"

There was quite a lengthy pause. So I addressed myself again to the young man who considered himself in love. "There's another drawback to this philosophy of yours," I said. "Suppose you fall out of love and don't get married. Do you think your girl will be just as attractive and desirable to somebody else after her love affair with you? Or will she seem a little secondhand? I've noticed that the men who are very broad-minded about their own premarital behavior still prefer girls who have been a lot less broad-minded. And why not? Put yourself in the place of the man who may eventually marry this girl of yours. Wouldn't you resent the faceless person—or persons—who had preceded you? Look back at that neat little checklist of yours and see if one of the requirements isn't a girl who hasn't been used as a sparring partner by other men. Am I right? Be honest now!"

"You're right," he said. "But chances are that I will marry this girl, once we're both out of college. And then everything will be all right!"

"Maybe it will," I said, "and maybe it won't. You've just admitted that one of your requirements for a wife is that she have high standards where sex is concerned. But you've also implied that you expect her to abandon those standards where you are concerned. Later on, after you're married, those elastic standards may come back to haunt you. You may even find yourself wondering if you can really trust your wife."

The boy smiled and said he couldn't conceive of such a thing. But I can. More than once I have been called on to deal with cases where premarital relations led to psychopathic jealousy later on.

Only a few months ago a pretty young woman came to me complaining bitterly about her husband's overpossessiveness and morbid suspicions. "I can't do anything," she said. "I can't dance with another man or even have a conversation without being accused of flirting. My husband is suspicious of every letter I get, every phone call. He's even suspicious of the milkman!"

"Well," I asked her, "has he anything to be suspicious about?"

"No!" she said vehemently. "Nothing. There's never been anyone else. There never will be. I tell him that, but he won't believe me."

"All right," I said. "I'll talk to your husband." And I did. I asked him what grounds he had for his jealousy. At first he denied that he was jealous. Then, when I refused to accept this, he tried to laugh it off. His wife was very attractive, he said. He knew that most men were potential wolves. He just wanted to make sure that there was no trouble.

"It seems to me," I said, "that you don't have much faith in your wife. Why not?"

He scowled and stared at the floor.

"Tell me something," I said. "Am I right in assuming that you two were lovers before you were married?"

He looked up defiantly. "What if we were? We got married, didn't we?"

"Yes," I said. "But you thought your conduct was wrong, even at the time. And now, right now, something in your unconscious is whispering to you that if your wife was willing to break the moral code with you, she might easily do it with somebody else. Isn't that the case?"

I have seldom seen a man grow so angry. "No!" he shouted. "Why do you say that?"

"Because I've run into this situation before," I told him. "Once Branch Rickey of the Dodgers asked me to help him with one of his baseball players. This man, a big-league pitcher, was so jealous of his wife that he could think of nothing else. He'd go to the telephone in the clubhouse between innings and call home to make sure that she was there, that she wasn't out cheating on him somewhere. This obsession was ruining him as a big-name athlete. Our psychiatrists at the clinic linked it to this same thing: premarital sex relations, followed by a sense of guilt and self-condemnation that builds up into morbid suspicions of the married partner. You might try comparing yourself to that man. As far as I can see, your symptoms are exactly like his."

My visitor stared at me for ten long seconds. Then he took a deep breath. "Maybe you've got something there," he said. "I'll think about it."

Evidently he did think about it, because his wife told me a few months later that their life together was much happier and more normal. But they both paid quite a price for their inability to wait for the marriage ceremony, and I imagine there are many couples like them.

When I encounter a case like this, I'm always struck by how harsh the psychological penalties can be for mistakes in this area of sexual behavior. That's why, over and over again in my discussions with young people, I find myself saying in one way or another, "Look, you're fascinated by sex, you're experimenting with sex, but you don't seem to have any realization of how serious a thing it is. You think it's a thrill you can take or leave, like a ride on a roller coaster. How can I make you see that it's infinitely more important than that, so important that it deserves the very best you can bring to it in terms of intelligence and thought and control? It's *not* like any other experience. For one thing, if mistakes are made, they can't be corrected easily. As William Graham Cole puts it in one of his books, 'Stolen goods can be returned, or compensated for, lies can be retracted and corrected, covetousness can be overcome. Even idolatry can be undone and forgiven. But the sex act once committed with another person cannot be undone. The inter-personal relationship has undergone a radical change, and the couple concerned can never return to where they were before. Something indelible has stamped them both.'

"What does this mean? It means that sex is an area where you really can't afford to be casual or careless, an area where if you have any wisdom at all you will look and look and look again before you leap."

Heaven knows this advice is not easy to follow. Pressure to leap first and look afterward comes from every point of the compass, and some of those pressures are ones that my generation never even dreamed of when we were in college. Probably the strangest—and saddest—reason I ever heard given for the increase in promiscuity on American campuses came from a college professor whose judgment I respect. He said that a lot of it represents an effort on the part of these young people to prove to themselves or their colleagues that they do not have homosexual tendencies. He went on to say that at some colleges non-participation in casual sex is now so unusual that the abstainer is looked at askance as someone with deviant tendencies—else why should he or she abstain?

When I replied that I found this hard to believe, my friend showed me the report of a psychiatrist connected with one of our better-known universities. It concerned three boys—sophomores—who roomed together in a two-bedroom suite on the campus. Two of these boys brought girls to the rooms regularly for love-making purposes; in fact, it was understood that each one had two afternoons a week in which he and his girl of the moment could have the rooms to themselves. The third boy had no girl—at least not one who was such a pushover. This began to worry the other two. More and more openly they expressed contempt and amazement that their friend's conduct of his sex life did not parallel their own.

Here is the psychiatrist's summary of what happened: "One day they taunted him until he agreed to be 'fixed up,' and a tryst was arranged with a girl who had been primed ahead of time to exert her seductive charms to the fullest and thus lure him into a sexual experience. As might be expected, the student found himself impotent in this situation for which he was neither emotionally nor sexually ready. He brooded about his failure and became increasingly convinced that he was hopelessly perverted. His roommates eventually became concerned enough about his state of mind to take him to a psychiatrist. Treatment was successful in restoring this boy to emotional health and averting what might have been a tragic end." The report added that such a case is typical of many that are seen in college health clinics each year.

I must say, the report left me thinking some dark thoughts about that particular university and the people involved in this sordid and tragic business. How did the boy's two roommates feel when they saw what happened to him? Did it make them think at all about the consequences of their pathetically oversimplified and animalistic approach to sex? Did any of the college authorities stop to wonder if a policy that permitted physically mature but emotionally immature youngsters to entertain girls in their rooms at their convenience was, after all, such a good thing? On a deeper level, did it occur to anyone that this center of learning, supposedly among the best in the land, was falling down in the area where it is supposed to excel, namely, education? These young men had to be intelligent to gain admission to the university in the first place. Did the thought cross anyone's mind that perhaps, where the whirlwinds of sex are concerned, intelligence is not enough, that there must also be restraints? Was anyone led to wonder, just for a moment, if possibly a course or two in self-discipline or self-control or even practical religion might be a badly needed part of the curriculum?

Listen to what V. A. Demant, an Oxford Professor of Moral Theology, has to say about this: "It has been the greatest error of the rational humanism of the last three centuries to believe that reason could master the passions, even reason in the service of civilization. The fact is that only when the passions are looked after, directed and catered for, by the deep, mysterious and worshipful forces of religious faith and ritual, can the top-story of human life be free to master itself by rational purpose and enquiry."

I think this is profoundly true. But I also think that in the general revolt against authority which is the hallmark of our troubled times, people—especially young people exposed to the "rational humanism" of our great universities—have drifted away from the church and no longer look to it for the kind of guidance that Canon Demant has in mind.

One reason for this, I'm sure, is that down through the ages the theology of sex has been primarily negative. The emphasis has been on the minuses of sex laxity, not on the pluses of sexual self-control. This approach worked fairly well so long as people were content to accept the wisdom and authority of the church in the realm of morals. But once they began to question that wisdom and that authority, the negative approach began rapidly to lose its effectiveness.

As I have indicated before in this book, the more I deal with people, the more aware I become of the limitations of the "Don't" approach. I know that every minister, every guidance counselor, must use it sometimes. Indeed, most of the arguments I have set forth so far in this chapter are negative rather than positive.

But whenever I use these purely negative arguments—in a sermon, let's say—to persuade people to control their sex lives, I have the feeling that I'm missing a large part of my audience. To be sure, negative arguments do *some* good; they find a receptive target here or there. But they also glance off many people who feel uneasily and resentfully that when you argue negatively about sex you are trying to restrain them, hinder them, take something desirable away from them. And they're likely to shrug the whole thing off by saying to themselves, "Well, after all, he's a preacher; he's got to talk like that!"

Is there a positive argument that you can offer such people? Yes, there is. It's the argument that to get the most out of sex you *have* to be selective, you *have* to be fastidious, you *have* to be controlled. It's the argument that promiscuity kills intensity where sex is concerned.

I am absolutely convinced that this is true. In my forty-odd years as a minister I have counseled with literally hundreds of men and women who have kept reaching for sex satisfaction with one partner after another, and my sober conclusion is this: if it's depth of emotion that you are looking for in love-making, or even the maximum degree of physical sensation, you cannot disperse your emotional and physical energies, or divide, or dilute them. You must concentrate them. Sex at the right place and the right time with the right person under the right circumstances is just about the most tremendous experience human beings can know. But in our society this means sex under the seal and shield of marriage. Under any other circumstances it is likely to be clumsy, guilt-ridden, limited, and spiritually enervating.

Recently a college girl I know who is very close to her father wrote him a letter telling him how prevalent casual sex was among her classmates. She said that the pressure to discard her moral standards came not only from young men, which she expected, but also from "open-minded" girls who had joined the ranks of the black sheep and apparently were made uneasy by the presence of a white one. There was more than one group, she said, where the requirement for acceptance, quite openly, was having "gone all the way" . . . the old, destructive "peer pressure" again. "They make it all sound so natural and so inevitable," she wrote, "that there are times when I wonder what I'm waiting for."

Her father was an understanding man, and a wise one. He replied: "I think I can tell you in six words what you are waiting for. You are waiting to be free. Free from the nagging voice of conscience and the gray shadow of guilt. Free to live all of yourself, not a panicky fraction. I know you pretty well and I know that the fastidious and perfectionist part of you has always wanted the best, not the second best. That's why you are such a wonderful person. And that's why you're holding out. Something in you, some deep instinct, knows what a tremendous experience your first complete union with another person can be—and that same instinct keeps telling you not to blur it, not to waste it, not make it small." And he added, in a wry postscript, "Tell your broad-minded friends (good adjective for them!) not to be so broad-minded that their brains fall out!"

This argument that sexual restraint leads ultimately to sexual intensity and depth is one that many young people will accept, because it offers them a glorious plus, not a gloomy minus. And it's a highly personal reward. I believe, myself, that the sexual restraints devised by society are an unconscious manifestation of the wisdom of the human race —they deepen erotic power by controlling and focusing it, and the resulting energy drives mankind upward along the path of civilization. But this concept is too cold and remote for most people. They want to know what rewards sexual control has for them. Well, this is the answer: it gives them far greater intensity of experience in this, the most intense of all experiences.

Of course waiting can be difficult; all forms of self-control are. But self-denial in the present in order to gain greater benefits in the future is the hallmark of a rational human being. Besides, the fact that it is difficult will not necessarily discourage youngsters if you put it to them straight. They're stimulated by challenge. They like to be tested. They want some one to say to them, "I dare you!"

No matter how cynical or hard-boiled they seem at times (and often this is only a mask for uncertainty), young people are really far less disillusioned, far more idealistic than older people. They may turn away if you urge them to be moral, because the word, unfortunately, has negative connotations for many of them. But they will listen if you challenge them to take charge of their lives, to be bold and resolute, to govern themselves with a strong and disciplined will. The idea of self-mastery has a tremendous appeal for them—look at the Spartan austerity of many young athletes. They are not dismayed by obstacles. They take pride in attempting the difficult, and they know what you mean if you talk to them about the sense of inner strength and confidence that comes from achieving it.

They also know, deep down in their hearts, that casual sex is always self-oriented, and they do not really want to be self-centered or selfish. It is to this idealism and fastidiousness in youth, to their hunger for intensity of living and their willingness to respond to challenge that we ministers and parents and counselors should be making our appeal far more strongly than we do. This is the positive approach, and it will win far more converts than any negative one.

So far in this chapter I have dealt mainly with the problems of unmarried people because I believe that sex attitudes are formed early in life and that it's important to try to reach young people at the critical point where they are ready to break away from traditional external authorities and are groping for self-discovered standards of their own. But unmarried people are not the only ones driven by the whirlwinds. The Kinsey Report indicated that about 25 percent of married women and 50 percent of married men in this country are unfaithful at one time or another—and I think it highly probable that these percentages have risen since the report was published.

These are frightening figures if you believe, as most of us do, that infidelity is probably the greatest single threat to any marriage, and that marriage is the cornerstone on which civilization rests. What is wrong here? What can we say to these unhappy people?

Because that's what they are: unhappy. I don't mean simply that unfaithfulness makes them unhappy, although my observation has been that sooner or later it does. No, I think that usually it's unhappiness that makes them unfaithful. Looking back through the years, I can recall very few cases in my counseling work where unfaithfulness was the result of ungovernable passion or the uncontrolled physical desire of a person for some one not his married partner. Almost always, it seems to me, extramarital sex is a symptom, a reflection of some kind of basic emptiness in the life of the person who is attracted to it. It's almost as if such people thought that in illicit sex they could find the answer to the deep frustrations in their own lives: their lack of importance, their lack of success, their lack of closeness with their mates, their lack of religious conviction, their lack of fulfillment as human beings.

Perhaps in a few cases—let's face it—such people do find outside of marriage a kind of warmth and closeness, an ego-prop, a momentary escape from anxiety, a narcotic that dulls the pain of inadequacy. Sex, even misdirected sex, can offer these things.

But it's too much like the courage that the weakling finds in a bottle. To stay brave, you have to keep on drinking. And finally, whether you like it or not, reality comes crashing in. I have seen the same thing happen, many times, to unhappy people who try to use sex as a narcotic.

I might say here, in passing, that I think that in their

zeal to condemn extramarital sex, many ministers and counselors over-look the fact that sex inside of marriage can sometimes be as exploitive and selfish and destructive—as sinful, really—as sex outside of it. If either married partner uses the other person only to gratify personal desires, if either one uses sex as a weapon, or withholds it as a punishment, or demands it unilaterally, it seems to me that this is just as immoral as the misuse of sex outside of matrimony. Marriage is not a license for sex-selfishness. This is something that even happily married couples would do well to stop and think about occasionally.

Just as one can offer countless warnings about the dangers of premarital sex experimentation, so can one point out endlessly the destructive aspects of adultery. Indeed, the woman whose story I told at the beginning of this chapter did just that. She spoke, you remember, about the emotional dislocation that so often results when "emancipated" ideas about sex in the conscious mind collide with moral convictions that have sunk deep into the unconscious mind. She talked about the dangers to innocent and well-loved children. About the erosion of self-respect. About the dissipation and diffusion of vital energies.

And there's a further point that she did not make. If one extramarital adventure doesn't give basic satisfactions—and it's almost impossible for a clandestine love affair to do so —then it becomes easier and easier to chase the will-o'-the-wisp in another. Why not? Conscience is usually blunted. Deception becomes a habit. Opportunities arise when a person is looking for them. Most states of mind move progressively; promiscuity is no exception. The path leads on and on, and down and down.

I have heard it said by cynics that marriage is really an artificial state of affairs, that man (and woman too) is basically a polygamous animal. I don't believe this. I think there is in most people a deep, idealistic yearning that makes them want to be faithful, to have exclusive intimacy with one person and one person only. The institution of marriage recognizes this—it does not merely try to compel it. Wild geese, I'm told, mate for life and are faithful unto death. Can man's true instinct be weaker than a bird's?

Here are the thoughts of Morton M. Hunt, a shrewd observer, on this point: "This is why the occasional experiments in liberalized or permissive marriage, in which each partner is free to indulge in outside affairs, have so generally come to grief, engendering bitterness or misery in at least one of the partners; it is also why the key-swapping parties of certain suburban communities begin as sophisticated lechery, but shortly generate alcoholism, neurosis, divorce, and even murder. Several marriage counselors have told me of a number of cases in which one-night wife exchanges that began as mere half-drunken hedonism ended in a double divorce and double remarriage of the adulterous partners to each other."

Here again, it seems to me, the moral is plain, the moral that has run through pronouncements on sex for the last three thousand years: sex is too powerful, too profound, too elemental a force to be treated lightly or casually. It's like nitroglycerin—useful so long as it is protected and safeguarded, deadly if it is mishandled or abused.

Another drawback to extramarital sex is that it can never be complete. It is always partially blocked. One basic purpose of sex relations, obviously, is to create new life, bring children into the world. In extramarital sex this supreme privilege becomes a nightmarish source of anxiety and fright. Another basic purpose of sex is to symbolize giving of one's self to the other person. But in an affair there can be no such complete giving; it is always partial or conditional, hedged about with restrictions and reservations. In a Catholic pamphlet on sex education that I read recently, a Jesuit priest, Francis L. Filas, puts it calmly and lucidly: "Sexual acts outside of marriage," he writes, "are evil, partly because they have no meaning. Outside of marriage, too, they are against reason, for they attempt to symbolize a complete giving at a time when the state of complete giving—marriage—does not exist."

Furthermore, extramarital sex always weakens intramarital sex, and with it the heart of the marriage. Says Canon Demant: "If people experience the act of venereal union outside marriage, either for alleged experimental skill or to express trivial and passing emotions, or for fun, or in order to appear uninhibited and sophisticated, then you render the act less capable of being the root of married love; it ceases to be the expression of true personal union between man and wife." Or as a surgeon I know once put it dryly, "It's like using a scalpel to cut out paper dolls. You can cut out the paper dolls, all right, but you can't later do surgery with it."

All these arguments for confining sex to marriage make sense. All of them are intelligent, logical, true. And all of them will be useless if the emotional starvation inside a marriage reaches the point where one partner or the other begins to look for fulfillment elsewhere. That is why the true role of the minister or counselor lies, I think, not so much in denouncing infidelity as in helping people to make their marriage so strong, so satisfying, so rewarding that even the thought of being unfaithful is blotted out as unnecessary and unwarranted and just plain stupid.

That, I know, is what I try to do when I am called upon to try to salvage a marriage on the rocks. I try to make people see that if they can learn to be generous, patient, loving, and kind inside their marriages—in other words, self-controlled—these same qualities will be reflected back to them. I try to make them understand that the word freedom doesn't mean freedom to discard all rules, be selfish, be self-destructive; it means freedom to develop inner controls that gradually replace outer controls as a person moves through life and through ascending stages of maturity. I try to make them realize that, far from being merely restrictive, or merely deterrent, religion can fill up the gaps in empty lives by providing the kind of emotional security and resources and personal power that people can never find in the labyrinths of experimental sex.

Earlier in this chapter I said that very often people needed more than pious exhortation or stern condemnation to help them channel and control the dynamo of sex. Sometimes they need specific techniques that they can study and apply when the going gets tough. Here are six quite simple suggestions that may be helpful.

1. Acknowledge the power of sex. Countless people have gotten into deep water by assuming that they could control it and then blundering into situations where they *couldn't* handle it. Remember the nitroglycerin analogy, and act accordingly.

2. Look ahead. In just about any immoral action, the long-term disadvantages outweigh what seem to be the momentary advantages. This is doubly true in sex relationships. If you can train yourself to look at the probable consequences of some contemplated sex adventure, very often your instinct for self-preservation will come to your rescue.

3. Be honest with yourself. If you are involved in sex outside marriage, examine your motives and see if you can feel proud of them. Are you using another person to gratify your own desires—or worse, to conceal your own inadequacies from yourself? If you're a married man, must you have a sense of conquest to sustain a shaky ego? If you're a married woman, are you trying to compensate for the emotional poverty of your marriage? Are you using sex as a refuge from anxiety, worry, cowardice, lack of achievement? Is it a cover-up for a deep sense of personal inadequacy?

Self-honesty in answering such questions is always difficult, and usually painful, but sometimes it can be the beginning of real maturity.

4. Make a commitment. This is the key, I think, to sanity in sex. You have to use your intelligence to discern the values of self-restraint. You have to be convinced that they represent a plus in the complicated equation of life. But then you have to decide firmly, in your mind, that you want those values for yourself, that you're going to have them, and that you're not going to let go of them. You have to make a pledge, a decisive act of will that comes from deep inside of you, and stick to it. External rules and authorities cannot extract this commitment from you; it must come from within. And only when it comes from within will you find that it works and that you can live up to it.

5. Make this commitment in advance. There's no use waiting until a crisis is on your doorstep. By that time your judgment and control may be so affected that you will be unable to make a commitment, much less honor one. I remember once talking to a famous movie star in Hollywood whose long and happy marriage to one woman was a source of much wonderment in the celluloid capital. I knew that this man was constantly surrounded by beautiful women, many of whom threw themselves at him. So I asked him how he handled the problem. "Well," he said, "years ago when I married my wife I made a decision to look straight ahead from then on. Not to the right. Not to the left. Just straight ahead. And so when these situations arise, that's what I do. I don't turn my head even a fraction of an inch, because if I did I'd be lost. I just look straight down the road and keep going."

That man made a commitment where sex is concerned, and

he kept it, and he's one of the happiest and most successful men I know.

6. Respect the established moral codes. Nothing I have said about the importance of inner disciplines, of seeking and finding your own values, should be construed as a rejection of the ancient moral truths of religion. In fact, the deeper you go into your quest for self-mastery, the more you will find yourself returning to these old time-tested rules. I always smile when I hear some intelligent and eager youngster explain that where morals are concerned he has thrown off the shackles of the past and is on his way to create his own brave new world of freedom. If he is really intelligent, really honest, in the end his brave new world will include all the wisdom and all the restraints of the old.

Perhaps the methods of teaching these ancient truths need to be improved. Perhaps the old rules need to be made acceptable in new ways. But a new moral code altogether? Who would write it? Who would invent it? The police? The Bar Association? A convocation of professors? Nonsense! Life writes the moral code; it always has and it always will. God sets man upon the earth, gives him freedom of choice, and says to him, "Choose! Will you choose selflessness or selfishness? Morality or immorality? Discipline or disorder? It's up to you!"

The choice is inescapable, and I am convinced that in this confused and complex area of sex conduct, self-discipline is the key. Not grim, authoritative, threatening rules from without, but patient, watchful, steady, intelligent responsibility from within. This is the only way to the highest intensity of feeling, to maximum creativity, to the self-respect on which true joy of living is based.

Here is the heart of the matter: sexual restraint does not mean deprivation; it means happiness in depth, the kind of happiness that Christ meant when He urged us to keep His commandments so "that my joy might remain in you, and that your joy might be full."

MEMO TO THE READER NO. 4

Try Being Yourself

The other day my wife said to me, "Norman, don't you think that very often when people get involved in these sex tangles—especially young people—it's because they're just following the crowd, adopting the lower group-standards around them instead of sticking to the higher standards that are inside of them?" She went on to talk about the pressures that push people into this kind of weak-willed conformity. She added that, in her opinion, this failure to be our true selves was one of the most fundamental dishonesties of all.

Let's discuss this for a moment.

God made each of us different, didn't He? Of all the billions of human beings in this world, no two have the same fingerprints, or the same personality. But instead of rejoicing in this individuality, very often we seem to do our darndest to get rid of it, throw it away. We go for a downgrading standardization of ourselves. We decide we must be one of the boys. We take this divine gift of uniqueness and water it down until it almost disappears.

This really is a form of immorality, because when we begin to reject our specialness we begin to lose our freedom. The conformist is not a free man. He has to follow the herd, and he has little or nothing to say about where the herd is going. He begins to lose the capacity to think and act for himself. Finally he gets to the point where he *hopes* someone else will tell him what to do, where he *likes* being led or driven. Then he's no longer a real person; he's a statistic.

Fortunately, there are always some people who finally rebel against this pressure to conform. I met one the other day, and it was a refreshing experience. He was a college youngster from Massachusetts, and he told me that he had been going with a crowd that made a fetish of being as sloppy and unwashed as they possibly could. They wore old khaki pants, sneakers with no socks, and sweatshirts. It was considered a venial sin to get a haircut and a cardinal one to take a bath.

"I went along with all this," the boy told me, "because it seemed to be the accepted thing to do. The dirty sneakers and no socks were a kind of status symbol. But one day, coming down the corridor, I caught sight of a seedy-looking tramp coming the other way. And when I got close to him, I realized that this was no tramp—it was my own reflection in a mirror at the end of the hallway!

"Well, that shook me up quite a bit. That tramp wasn't the real me—at least, I hoped it wasn't. So I said to myself, 'Why don't you try being yourself for a change, instead of what you think other people expect you to be?' I went and had my hair cut. I took a bath. I put on a shirt and tie and jacket and some decent shoes and socks. And I felt like a new person. When I met my friends, they looked at me as if I'd just come down from Mars. 'What's with you?' they wanted to know. 'I'm just sick of being a phony,' I told them. 'This is the way I am, and from now on this is the way I'm going to be.' "

Be yourself—surely that challenge reaches close to the heart of this whole problem of responsibility. It takes courage, certainly. It takes will power. It takes a conscious and deliberate decision to stop worrying about what "they" may think or "they" may say. But once you make this decision, the rewards are tremendous. A feeling of power and exhilaration will sweep over you because you will know that you are no longer a slave to convention, or to non-conformity. You are the unique, uncopiable self that the Creator intended you to be. You are free!

So take a long look at yourself, especially at the areas where the image you try to project is not the real you. Do you pretend to be deeply interested in symphonic music when actually you prefer jazz? Do you laugh at off-color jokes when the inner you, the fastidious you, really shrinks away from that sort of thing? Do you drive a bigger car than you can afford because some deep insecurity whispers that this may impress the neighbors? Do you find yourself telling stories or anecdotes in which you exaggerate the role you played because you're afraid the real you doesn't impress people sufficiently?

If you want to reach the shining goal of true self-responsibility you must look for these areas of phoniness within yourself and root them out, one by one. This is one of the fundamental steps in the disciplines that lead to spiritual growth and emotional maturity.

And strangely, wonderfully, if you decide to be yourself, you will find that the real you is far more impressive, far more competent, far more alive, than any of the false images. You will no longer be an uneasy actor on the stage of life. You will be a vibrant, integrated, outgoing human being, because you will be expressing the uniqueness that was given to you at birth, your priceless heritage as a child of God.

There is one area of living, though, where people have to yield some of their individuality and yet, at the same time and in a mysterious way, keep it. That area is marriage, the most rewarding and the most demanding relationship on earth. Let's take a look, now, at the ancient institution of matrimony, see how it is faring in the moral revolution that surrounds us, and consider what self-discipline and inner-directedness can do to strengthen it.

CHAPTER VI

Marriage: Control or Chaos

The theme of this book—admittedly a hopeful theme—is that we are moving away from a past in which people were controlled mainly by external rules or legalisms toward a more enlightened future in which people will finally learn how to control themselves.

The purpose of this book—admittedly an optimistic purpose—is to enable people to see the necessity for such inner-directedness and to help them acquire it.

But no amount of optimism can or should disguise the fact that this period of transition is a difficult one. As the old restraints drop away, confusion, uncertainty, at times even elements of anarchy seem to creep in. When laws are removed, there is bound to be a period of relative lawlessness before a new order is established. To put it another way, whenever a society (or an individual) reaches out for full maturity, the growing pains are often sharp and unpleasant.

One area where the growing pains are all too evident is the institution of marriage. Not long ago, out in California, I came upon some dramatic, if depressing, proof of this. I happened to open the San Diego *Union* to the page where marriage license applications and divorces are listed. To my astonishment, the number of names in each list looked so nearly equal that I counted them to see which was running more strongly—the trend into marriage or the trend out of it.

A total of 106 marriage licenses had been issued. There were 104 couples,—or rather, ex-couples—listed under "Divorces Filed," "Interlocutory Decrees," and "Final Decrees." Actually, one of the happy pairs securing a license had been married to each other before, so the margin was even slimmer than it seemed at first glance. "Marriages," said Tennyson, "are made in Heaven." Maybe so, but certainly a great many of them are being unmade on earth.

And what does this mean? It means, again, that the rules and restraints that once governed our society have grown progressively weaker—and that the inner disciplines which must replace them are not yet strong enough, in many people, to create successful marriage.

In many cases that I see in my counseling work, this lack of inner discipline is incredible. The other day a young woman came to see me, pretty, well-dressed, a bit sulky. She said her husband wasn't making her happy. She was thinking about getting a divorce.

"What's wrong with your husband?" I asked her. "Does he drink too much?"

"No, he doesn't drink much."

"Does he beat you?"

"No."

"Is he unfaithful?"

"No," she said. "He just doesn't make me happy."

I looked at this child-woman sitting there in her elegant clothes. "Is your husband well educated?"

"Oh, yes," she said. "He went to a very good college."

I felt my patience end with an almost audible snap. I stood up and looked down at her. "Young woman," I said, "do you think that God Almighty created this man solely to provide you with happiness? Do you think his parents struggled and sacrificed to educate him just so that he could placate a spoiled little self-centered kitten like you? What are you contributing to life that makes you deserve this happiness you're so concerned about? A person shouldn't marry just for idyllic happiness so much as to be an honest-to-God partner with another human being. You want my advice? All right, here it is. Go away and try to find some humility and unselfishness and responsibility in yourself. When you do, come back and I'll talk to you!"

She went away, looking stunned. Whether or not she'll take my advice I don't know. But unless she takes it, I'm pretty sure she'll choose the line of least resistance in her marriage—the easy out known as divorce.

A hundred years ago, she would have had no such choice. In those days the divorce rate in this country was only a fraction—less than one-seventh—of what it is today. People considered divorce a violation of the laws of God. All churches condemned it. Few ministers would consider remarrying a divorced person. Social ostracism was a real and feared penalty; in many places a divorced woman was considered little better than a prostitute. Most wives were bound to their husband, in any case, by economic ties; they had no means of livelihood outside of marriage. Most important of all was the attitude of people who got married. They assumed that it was for keeps, that they couldn't get out, that the relationship would endure, for better or worse, until death. And so most of the time they knuckled down and made it work.

Today, of course, if things go badly, people assume that they can get out—and many do. Some eight hundred thousand persons are divorced every year in the United States alone. Since about three million Americans are married each year, this means that roughly one in four ventures into matrimony is going to wind up officially on the rocks—and this doesn't include the estimated one million separations or the one hundred thousand desertions that take place annually. The most tragic statistic of all is that thirteen million children are growing up in broken homes.

Now which is better—a system in which people stay married no matter what, or one in which divorce becomes almost as easy as marriage itself? There is no quick or simple answer. A century ago there must have been plenty of unhappy and maladjusted marriages that staggered along in bitterness and hatred to the end. Was such an atmosphere better for the children than the cold and ruthless surgery of modern divorce? Who knows? In any case, what difference does it make? Neither a loveless marriage nor a divorce is anything but a crashing failure in one of the most critical areas of living. Both leave a permanent smudge on the human soul. And both happen, I'm convinced, when people fail to display the qualities that we are talking about in this book: self-discipline, self-responsibility, self-control.

Believe me, the marriage counselor or the minister who tries to help shaky marriages is up against a tough job. Matrimony is probably the most difficult as well as the most rewarding of all relationships. It makes enormous demands on people, often before they are mature enough to handle such demands. The need for patience and tolerance and adjustment never ceases. The daily requirements of sacrifice and selflessness never grow less. No wonder, knowing the centrifugal forces within any marriage, society used to chain two people together and throw away the key!

But that too-simple solution has been abandoned, now. In this area, as in so many others, we have clamored for freedom and we have gotten it.

One positive and exciting thing about this freedom is that it cuts both ways. People are free now to get out of marriage, but they are also free to stay in. In the old days, wives *had* to minister to their husbands' needs—whether they wanted to or not. Now they can do it for love, freely, selflessly, with no compulsion, no chains.

It takes a wise and generous person to accept this freedom and react to it joyously and selflessly. It calls for true maturity—and there's the rub. Lack of maturity—that is to say, lack of emotional self-control—is at the bottom of 90 percent of all marital problems.

Time and again I have seen married couples come to the brink of divorce for reasons so absurd that you wonder how they got through high school! Such a young couple sat in my office not long ago rigid with fury and hurt pride. And what were their grievances? He was enraged because his wife refused to bake him the kind of lemon meringue pie his mother had always made. (She said loudly that she refused because she was not going to have her cooking compared unfavorably to her mother-in-law's.) Her grievance was that he always left the bathroom in a mess, towels on the floor, clothes lying around, "a white-tiled pig-sty!" she called it. (He said loudly that it was the woman's job to keep the house in order.)

I felt like taking them both by the scruff of the neck and shaking them. "Listen," I said, "you two have got to grow up and grow up fast. Physically you may be adults, but emotionally you're still children, expecting every day to be Christmas and sulking when it isn't! You, young man, evidently had a doting mother who treated you like a baby, picking up after you, cooking special dishes for you. You're still acting like a baby! And you, young lady, could easily cope with these so-called crises if you knew anything about managing a man, which is what you signed on to do in the first place!"

They both looked somewhat abashed.

"Now," I said to the wife, "I'm going to suggest a profound solution to both these earth-shaking problems. Where the bathroom is concerned, if he makes it into a mess, leave it a mess. Don't pick up a thing until he shows a reasonable degree of tidiness. As for the lemon pie, go ahead and bake it, on two conditions: first, that he promise not to mention his mother's cooking in any way whatsoever, and second that he eat every crumb of it at one sitting, whether it's any good or not!"

They both smiled at that, and I felt a bit encouraged. If a sense of humor has survived in a marriage, I've found, much else can usually be salvaged. I went on to tell them that neither should expect miraculous changes overnight, but that each had to learn to work on their own shortcomings and be more tolerant of their partner's. "One sign of maturity," I told them, "is recognition of the fact that all people have flaws, including you. Another is the ability to learn from past mistakes. So go on home and start learning. You'll be happy if you do, miserable if you don't. It's as simple as that!"

It's not really simple at all. Replacing self with selflessness never is; it's so difficult that the Bible compares it to being born again. There is no easy prescription. There is only one rule that applies in virtually every case: control yourself. That is the secret: control, control, control.

Not long ago a young married couple came to me with one of the most common of all marital complaints. "What's the matter with us?" they said bewilderedly. "We're in love, but we have terrible fights. We're afraid they're undermining the foundations of our marriage. What can we do?"

"You can do a lot of things," I told them. "First of all, you can stop thinking that romantic love is going to keep you from fighting or solve all your difficulties. It won't. The truth is, being 'in love' is a far cry from loving another person wholeheartedly and unselfishly. People 'in love' are often much more concerned with their own feelings than the welfare or happiness of the person they're 'in love' with. So get your thinking straight on that.

"Next, expect a few fights. When I hear people say, as I sometimes do, that they have lived together for forty years without a single argument, I think they must either be very forgetful, or else they are paper dolls, not people. What a pallid, dull existence!

"Of course you're going to have differences of opinion and disagreements! We're all human beings, not angels. There are times when each of us is cross or worried or tired, when the threshold of irritability is low. When such times in the lives of two married people coincide, sparks are likely to fly.

But this is nothing to be alarmed about; sometimes a good shower of emotional sparks clears the air and leads to better understanding all around. Besides, there's always the pleasure of making up! In my own marriage, I think that is one of the things I've enjoyed the most.

"The real goal in marriage," I told them, "is not to eliminate all quarrels; it's to have civilized ones rather than brutal, hurtful ones that leave permanent scars. And there are specific, definite things to keep in mind. For instance, try to keep the difference of opinion at the discussion—not the argument—level. Keep your voice down. If the heat begins to build up, speak in a whisper: it's very difficult to carry on a violent argument in a whisper! Look down at your hands. Are you gripping the arm of the chair? Relax! Are your fingers clenched? Uncurl them! Before you hurl your next verbal bombshell, take ten deep breaths—this is better than simply counting to ten."

I went on to tell them, a bit wryly, that in giving them this sage advice I was also preaching at myself. When Ruth and I disagree as we sometimes do, I have a tendency to wave my arms and cry, "Why do we always fight?" "We're not fighting," she says in a calm and matter-of-fact voice. "We're having a discussion." And since it takes two to make a real fight, she's usually right. Incidentally, beware of that word 'always.' If you start telling your married partner that he or she 'always' does this, or 'always' does that, it's a sign that you are losing your own emotional control.

I also cautioned my young visitors about the importance, when they did fight, of fighting fair. Everyone has areas of sensitivity, of vulnerability, and there is always a strong temptation to strike at these weak spots, whether the argument is concerned with them or not. Such thrusts can be terribly cruel, they can drive right through the pitifully thin armor that most of us wear, and inflict hideous wounds. Often they silence the opposition. But having the last word in an argument, I sometimes think, is proof that you have lost it. If you have wounded your adversary so grievously that he has no reply at all, you must have thrown away your self-control and your sense of fair play to do it. Believe me, this is no victory.

My final advice to this young couple was to pray together about their areas of friction. This was not simply because I am a minister, or because I believe in unloading all human problems on God. It was because, in case after case, I have seen this technique of bringing a problem before the highest bar of justice raise the whole matter out of the swamps of anger and bitterness to emotional high ground where the healing forces of reason and selflessness begin to work on it. As I said to them, prayer is like a lightning rod that deflects harmful emotions into an area so vast that their destructive powers are swallowed up and lost.

In more than forty years of marriage counseling, I don't suppose I have ever made exactly the same recommendations twice, because people are infinitely complex, and no two cases are alike. But recalling the exhortations and the warnings that I have given people through the years, it is apparent to me that all are variations on a set of principles designed to point out the areas of greatest danger in the marital relationship and the areas of greatest need. In the remainder of this chapter I should like to discuss these various recommendations, hoping that anyone who needs to do so will fit some or all of them to his own case. It will take self-honesty and self-discipline, but it can be done.

One of the greatest needs in any marriage, in my opinion, is the need for *balance*. Marriage is, or should be, a team effort in which the strengths of one partner balance the weaknesses of the other. But no team effort is possible if one partner insists on trying to run the whole show. Individuals with a strong drive to dominate make poor marriage partners because they are never satisfied with people as they are; they are forever trying to force them to conform with their idea of what they ought to be. In some marriages this takes the form of constant nagging. In others it degenerates into downright bullying. Neither has any place in a true partnership.

I have seen cases where strong action was required to bring some selfish or domineering person into line. During World War II, I remember, I was asked to officiate at the wedding of a young soldier and his bride. The girl's parents were both college professors—gentle, somewhat ineffectual people. Their daughter, an only child, apparently had been pushing them around for years. For after the wedding rehearsal, when her mother did or said something that displeased this girl, she flew into a temper, slapped her mother in the face, and stamped off to the hotel where they were all staying.

Everyone, naturally, was aghast. The fiancé, greatly upset, apologized to me and said he would bring the girl back to apologize. "If I were you," I told him, "I'd do more than that. I'd follow that girl back to the hotel, lock the door, put her over your knee, and give her the spanking she should have had a dozen years ago. And don't settle for love taps, either. She's like a colt that has to be broken. If you don't do this now, your married life won't be worth living."

"All right," he said grimly, "I'll do it." And he did. It was a rather subdued bride who said her vows the next day. But I still hear from them occasionally, and I know it has been a good marriage.

Probably the most drastic marital action of this kind that I ever heard of took place years ago when my father was Superintendent of a Methodist District in Ohio. A slight, frail woman was married to a rough, tough Irishman who had a habit of coming home drunk, abusing her and the children, and falling into bed in a stupor. Nothing my father or anyone else could say made any impression on him until one night the worm turned—with a vengeance. When her drunken husband passed out on the bed, the wife took her children to a neighbor's house. She came back, found a clothesline, and tied her husband hand and foot. She brought a buggywhip from the stables. She filled a bucket with water. She sloshed water on his head until he woke up. Then she lashed him unmercifully with the whip. The more he bellowed, the more she beat him, nor did she stop until he swore a solemn oath never to come home drunk again. Not only did he keep his promise, my father said, he was so proud of his wife's spunk that he went around telling the story on himself, shaking his head and saying, "What a woman! What a woman!"

I don't necessarily recommend actions as forthright as this, but that woman restored to her marriage the balance that I am talking about!

Another basic need in marriage stems from one of the deepest of all human cravings—the desire to be appreciated. The great psychologist, William James, once remarked ruefully that in his classic works on human personality he had failed to mention this yearning, and that it was perhaps the most universal craving of all.

Life for most of us is a series of tough and difficult problems; we need all the confidence and reassurance we can get. Nothing builds confidence and reassurance like a word of praise. Nothing restores our self-esteem and recharges our psychic batteries like a little admiration. Why, then, needing appreciation so badly ourselves, do we deny it so often to others? Why, indeed!

Sometimes when a husband or a wife comes to me complaining bitterly about their marriage partner, I ask them to write down a list of all their mate's shortcomings. They usually perform this task with alacrity. Then I ask them to write—opposite each accusation—a quality that they once admired, or still admire in the other person. Sometimes they are able thus to balance the books, sometimes not. But I've never yet encountered a case where the complainant was unable to find *something* good to say about the complainee! I then make them promise, within the next twenty-four hours, to say something complimentary about that particular characteristic to the owner of it. Very often this simple device proves to be a turning point in the whole relationship.

One man to whom I gave this advice carried it a step further. That evening at home he sat down near his wife with a pad and pencil, looked at her speculatively from time to time, and began to write.

"What are you doing?" she finally asked him.

"Writing a list of your good qualities," he said.

"Good qualities?" she echoed incredulously. "I didn't know you thought I had any!"

"Well, you do," he said, and went on writing. Pretty soon, being human, she asked to see them. He demurred, but finally yielded. She read what he had written with amazement and pleasure. "Why," she said, "I had no idea that anything about me pleased you any more."

"Lots of things do," he said cheerfully. "A few don't."

"Well," she said, "while you're at it, you'd better list those too."

"I will," he said, "if you'll do the same for me."

The upshot was that both of them got their grievances out in the open in such a calm and amicable way that they were able to resolve quite a few of them. As my grandmother Fulton used to say back in Ohio, there's more than one way to skin a cat!

A third great need in marriage is for mutual understanding. "Do not wax indignant," wrote Spinoza. "Do not resent—understand!" This dispassionate attitude can be very difficult to maintain; at times it requires an almost superhuman degree of self-control. But if, when things go wrong in your marriage, you can ask yourself *why*—instead of merely reacting with hostility or anger—you have a much better chance of finding the basic trouble and setting it right.

It's amazing how understanding can lessen exasperation even in trivial incidents. One night last summer I was unable to sleep because of the sound of electric motors in our neighbor's barn. I tossed and turned, fumed and fretted, and finally burst out with: "What's the matter with those people? Why are they running that machinery in the middle of the night?"

"Because they're drying their hay," Ruth said. "Those fans run all night to take the moisture out of the hay."

"Oh!" I said sheepishly. And as soon as I knew the reason, the annoyance went out of the noise and I went peacefully to sleep.

Deep understanding underlies the gentle and Christ-like quality that we call compassion. *"Tout comprendre,"* says the old French proverb, *"c'est tout pardonner*—to understand everything is to forgive everything." Perhaps this is not always literally true, but certainly if we try to understand why our marriage partners behave as they do we shall be less inclined to blame them for actions that displease us.

True understanding includes the knowledge that when things go wrong in a marriage the blame is never entirely one-sided. Sometimes it takes a lot of courage to face up to this. I remember a case brought to my attention by a business executive who was a friend of mine. One of his crack salesmen had become involved in a messy affair with his secretary. Somehow his wife had found out. She had not spoken to her husband since. The salesman was faced with the break-up of his marriage and possible loss of his job.

The executive persuaded each of them to come to my office. Just the four of us were there. The man admitted that what he had done was wrong. He said it was all over; that it would never happen again.

I asked the wife if she had anything to say. She was very pale, but very calm. "Yes," she said, "I have one question. Have there been any women before this one?"

The husband swore that there had not, that this was his only lapse. I believed him; he was too agitated to be telling anything but the truth. The executive made it plain that he was not interested in continuing to employ a philanderer. Unless the wife was willing to forgive the husband, he said, he was through with him.

That left everything up to the wife. I asked her what she wanted to do. "You have to decide right now," I told her. "Once you leave this room, you won't be able to change your mind. Or if you do, it will be too late."

She took a deep breath. "I've been hurt," she said. "My world has been shaken. But then, when was life ever a bed of roses? Perhaps we've had things too easy in the past. And part of this situation must be my fault. I must have failed somewhere. I shall try to change myself, do a better job as a wife. I will re-examine myself honestly!" How wise she was. She sensed the fact that without personality defects in her, this situation might never have developed. "Perhaps, somehow, we can try to rebuild something . . ."

"Let me warn you: if you forgive your husband now," I said to her, "you must never mention this episode again. You must lock the door on it and throw away the key."

"I know," she said. "That is my duty and my desire."

Duty and desire—it's not often you hear those words linked in a single sentence. It takes a deeply inner-directed person to do it. I put my hand on hers. "You're a great person," I said, "and I think you'll have your reward."

Actually, she already had it; I can still remember the love and gratitude in her husband's eyes, and the happiness in her own, as they went out together. A potential tragedy had been turned into an unprecedented closeness—and understanding was the key.

Sometimes, of course, understanding is difficult because the basic motivation for a person's behavior may be hidden deep in the unconscious mind. In such cases, professional psychiatric help may be necessary, and the sooner it is sought the better. Early in my counseling years I discovered that there were some people whom I could not help; my best efforts and their attempts to respond were blocked by hidden forces that were very powerful. It was this realization that led me to start a clinic at the Marble Collegiate Church in New York where psychiatrists and ministers could work together, a clinic that has since grown into the American Foundation of Religion and Psychiatry, with a staff of ninety people and an annual budget of some five hundred thousand dollars.

Every week dozens of marital problems are analyzed by the specialists at the foundation, often with a high degree of success. On my desk, for example, is a report on the case of a girl who behaved with normal sweetness and affection during her engagement, but who became—after her marriage— bitter and shrewish and hostile toward her husband. She acted as if she hated him—and for no valid reason.

Now, a well-meaning friend or even an untrained pastor might have spent a great deal of time investigating this woman's relationship with her husband, delving into his behavior, his personality, and so on. But that would have been wasted effort. It didn't take the psychiatrists long to discover that the roots of the problem were in the woman's childhood, when she had had to endure a harsh and repressive father who used to shout at his children, bully them, punish them unfairly. Once when this daughter summoned up the courage to protest, he slapped her in the face and ordered her out of the house. Soon after that, he died.

Much of the woman's bitterness had been suppressed and forgotten. But when she married her fiancé, *and he became "head of the house,"* all that latent fury was suddenly reawakened and directed against him. And until she gained insight into this unconscious identification, she was powerless to understand it or control it. The files at the Foundation are full of such cases, and the moral is plain: don't be too proud or too sensitive to seek help of this kind when you need it.

A fourth basic requirement in marriage, I think, is the need for realism. Thousands of people make themselves and their partners miserable because of too-great expectations. I have seen many wives try to drive their husbands far beyond their capabilities in their jobs or professions because these women had a fantasy-vision of financial or social success in their minds and could not or would not let go. This is a sign of great immaturity and insecurity. I have also seen many husbands try to goad their wives into activities for which they had neither the inclination nor the aptitude.

Realism in marriage, in other words, calls for acceptance; in many areas you have to *accept* your married partner as they are, not as you'd like them to be. You must take them as they are, love them as they are.

This acceptance, which in itself is a form of selflessness and self-control, sometimes brings more contentment than the desired change itself would bring. I thought of this not long ago when I was watching Mr. and Mrs. Casey Stengel being interviewed on television. It was their golden wedding anniversary, and Casey was celebrating it—as you might expect—by managing a baseball game. Mrs. Stengel remarked, with a twinkle, that at one point she had tried to instill a love of fine art into her husband. "I took him to Rome and Florence," she said, "and tried to get him to go to the art galleries. But all he did was stay in the hotel and talk baseball to the bellboys!"

Of course he did. He was being himself—a great baseball manager. And his wife had the good sense to leave him that way!

Not all married couples are so wise. I once knew a man who married a beautiful girl, one of the most stunning blondes I ever saw. He was wild about her, and when she agreed to marry him he considered himself the luckiest man alive. But on their honeymoon, he told me later, he got a terrible jolt. They were on an ocean liner, bound for Europe, and one night as they stood by the ship's railing in the moonlight he began to tell her how happy he was and how he visualized their future life together. He painted a glowing picture of domestic tranquility. He saw himself coming home from work to an adoring wife and children, sitting down to home-cooked meals, the whole fireside-slippers-and-pipe routine.

It was a pipe dream, all right. His beautiful bride drew back and looked at him as if he had lost his mind. Domesticity, she told him, was the last thing she wanted. She liked gaiety, excitement, parties. She had no interest in children; she would prefer the independence and challenge of a job. As for cooking, she loathed anything to do with kitchens. Nor did she intend to change.

Her husband was so shocked and dismayed that he never did get over it. He felt that he had been tricked, deceived. Later on, he began to solace himself with other women, and the marriage broke up. Here was a classic case that began with an almost unbelievable lack of communication and ended with total failure to adjust and compromise and react intelligently rather than emotionally to a problem. A classic case, in other words, of lack of realism.

One other aspect of marriage that doesn't get as much attention as it should is the need for good timing. Timing is the key to success in almost everything, from athletics to salesmanship, and marriage is no exception. How many domestic quarrels could be avoided if husband and wife would make a pact not to discuss explosive issues when either partner is tired or upset? How many marriages could be strengthened by a word of encouragement or affection at the moment when it's really needed?

Everyone encounters dips in the graph of living when they feel hypersensitive or irritable, when their reserves of patience and good humor are low, when they can't stand criticism or complaints. It pays to study your married partner and learn to recognize these moods. One elderly farm couple that I heard of worked out a set of signals early in their married life. If he was feeling grim or out of sorts, he rolled one pants leg up to his shin. If she was in a blue or vulnerable mood, she put her apron on backwards. It started as a joke, but they kept it up through the years and swore that it saved them from all sorts of unpleasantness.

Good timing isn't accidental or instinctive; it's a blend of imagination and awareness of other people's needs, and self-control. And like all self-disciplines, it pays great dividends to those who master it.

There are other important needs in marriage that do not require lengthy discussion because they are self-evident. The need for patience. The need for flexibility. The need for optimism—looking for the best instead of the worst in a given situation. The need for sharing—sharing ideas, interests, problems. The need for loyalty. These quiet, positive qualities are seldom dramatic, but in the long run they supply the oil that keeps the machinery of marriage running smoothly.

As for the negative, destructive attitudes that throw sand or monkey wrenches into the gears, I have found that there are several thorny things to beware of:

1. Jealousy, not just sexual jealousy (although that can be a cancer at the heart of any marriage), but the more subtle and deadly jealousy that married people sometimes feel for their partner's success or importance if it seems to exceed their own. I have known men who refused to let their wives take a job because their own self-esteem was too shaky to risk the chance that a woman might outshine them. I have seen women react with resentment and hostility to their husband's professional success because they feared they might somehow be excluded or left behind.

I knew a painter once whose wife was loyal and devoted—so long as he was obscure and unknown. But when he began to be a success, she could not stand the attention and acclaim that he got, although he tried to share it with her. She began to disparage him, slyly and silkily, in public. Whenever the subject of his painting came up, she would make veiled but biting references to his shortcomings in other fields. Finally, unable to endure her relentless animosity, he left her—and it was hard to blame him.

Such jealousy is often a reflection of a deep sense of insecurity. If you are the target of it, you have to give your partner the reassurance that he or she needs. If you're the source of it, you have to try to root this insecurity out of yourself. Both these remedies call for discipline, maturity, selflessness. But the effort is worth it, because in the end you get back far more than you put in.

2. Self-righteousness. Some of Our Lord's sternest rebukes were directed at people like the proud Pharisee who went around congratulating himself that he was not "as other men are." This sort of smugness is never justified. No one is perfect. Each of us has his faults. To make another person feel that you are morally better than he is not only insulting and infuriating—it may not even be true.

Very often a husband or wife will seize on some failing or transgression that their partner has been guilty of, contrast it with their own performance *in that particular area,* and thus justify all sorts of recriminations and reprisals. Such people should remember Jesus' admonition about plucking the beam out of your own eye before you worry about the mote in your neighbor's. Judge not, He said—unless you are prepared to be judged. Recrimination calls forth recrimination. Fault-finding provokes fault-finding. The universe is really an echo chamber in which you get back what you give, and the heart of the Christian message is that you must give love in order to receive it.

Today, twenty centuries after Christ, psychologists and psychiatrists are warning people not to be too critical because, they say, if a person is forever finding fault there is probably something wrong with *him.* Perhaps his disapproval of others is a mask for a deep-seated disapproval of himself. Perhaps he risks antagonizing people because something in him feels that he is not worthy of being liked. Perhaps his ego is so shaky that he can build himself up only by tearing other people down. In any case, it's an area where periodic self-examination is a good discipline for everyone, married or not!

3. Misplaced resentment. Called upon to face some frustration or disappointment, a person reacts with what seems to be admirable self-control at the time—but explodes later over some trifle. Very often in a marriage, this kind of pent-up anger will strike the married partner—almost as if some sort of emotional magnet were involved. And perhaps it is: psychiatrists tell us that lurking behind love there is always hate. Certainly when love dies it seems likely to be replaced by hate. Any divorce lawyer will bear witness to this. One of the grimmest remarks I ever heard in my life was made by a young woman whose marriage was on the rocks. She spat the words out like acid. "If you really want to learn to hate someone," she said, furiously, "marry them!"

Many tense and frustrated people find relief in physical activity that symbolically releases their pent-up anger or resentment. One politician I know keeps a punching bag in his cellar, and beats a tattoo on it every night before he goes to bed. One lady lawyer unwinds after a hard day in court by going for a walk in the country carrying a riding crop with which she joyously slices off the tops of weeds. Any sport in which you hit some inanimate object—golf, tennis, bowling—burns up aggressive feelings harmlessly. So does gardening; Kipling's advice to people in a bad humor, you remember, was to "take a large hoe, and a shovel also, and dig till you gently perspire."

In any case, it's neither intelligent nor fair to look for a scapegoat. If life deals harshly with you, fight back—don't just kick the cat!

I think, myself, that if you have some grievance or resentment it is far better to get it out in the open than to let it fester inside of you. A few months ago, after I gave a talk in Atlanta, I found a young couple waiting to see me. It was late, and I was tired, so I suggested that they drive me back to my hotel. They did.

As we drove along, the husband did most of the talking. He said that their marriage had started out well, but that now it was going very badly. Much of the time his wife was withdrawn and resentful. Their sex life had deteriorated; she seemed frigid and disinterested. They quarreled about trifles. I asked the wife if all this was true. She admitted in sub-

dued tones that it was. She added that most of it was her
fault.

"Well," I said, "something must be bothering you. When
people act this way it usually means that they're suffering
from one of three things: guilt, fear, or hate. Have you done
anything that you're ashamed of, that you can't bring yourself to admit to anyone?"

"No," she said.

"Are you afraid of anything?"

She shook her head.

"Do you hate anyone?"

She looked almost fearfully at her husband. "Can I say
what I really think? Just for once?"

He said that she could.

"I hate your mother," she burst out. "Yes, I hate her!
She interferes. She criticizes. She comes between us. I resent
her bitterly. And I resent you for letting her do these things,
never taking my side! I've never mentioned it before, but I
can't stand it any longer." And she began to weep.

"Well," I said, "go ahead and cry; it will do you good. It
just could be that your failure to become pregnant is related
to the tension which has been brought about by your hatred
of your mother-in-law.

"Now," I said to the girl, "I think there are two things
for you to do. The first is to declare your independence of
your mother-in-law. Let your husband go to see her whenever he likes—after all, she's his mother. But in your home
she must measure up to your standards of behavior. No
more criticizing. You have the right to insist on this, and
your husband must back you up." I glanced at him. "Will
you do this? Can you do it?"

He said that he thought he could.

"The other thing you must do," I said to the girl, "is try
to love your mother-in-law instead of hating her. I know you
think that's impossible, but it isn't really. Look at it like this:
as long as you hate a person, they have power over you. They
can upset you. They can make your life miserable. They can
even ruin your marriage, as you well know. But if you love
them, they lose this power. They no longer control the situation; you do!

"Now when you go home, pray about this together. You've
verbalized your problem, and that's a good beginning. It lets
light and air into what was a dark, moldy closet in your soul.

Don't let the door swing shut again. Keep it open, and work on this thing together, and ask God to help you. He will!"

Twice since then I've had letters from them, saying that things are going much better—and all because a hidden resentment was brought out into the open where the healing forces of kindness and understanding could work on it and eliminate it. They have had a baby, and the mother-in-law's love for the grandchild has brought them all closer.

What if that grievance hadn't been eliminated? Would that marriage have ended in divorce? Very likely. Love is strong, but it is fragile, too. Sooner or later, sustained resentment will first cripple it, then paralyze it, and finally kill it. Marriage is such an intense relationship that there *must* be affection if it is to endure. Without it, the strains and stresses and frictions become intolerable.

I am convinced that in normal people the requirements for a happy marriage—understanding, tolerance, kindness, unselfishness—almost always exist in adequate quantities. It's when these qualities become stifled or blocked by lack of maturity, lack of self-discipline, lack of control that trouble begins. That is when anger takes over, communication begins to fail, grievances begin to be magnified out of all proportion, happy memories are brushed aside and forgotten. And unless corrective steps are taken, the marriage can easily pass the point of no return on the toboggan slide toward divorce.

More than once, when I have seen married couples approaching this point of no return, I have asked them to try an experiment that in some cases has produced remarkable results. Each of them has to agree to contribute half an hour a day for a period of a week, agree to follow directions, and agree to complete the experiment even though they may resist some parts of it at first.

If they do agree, I tell them to go into a quiet room where they will not be disturbed, set an alarm clock to ring in half an hour, place the clock where both can watch it, and divide the half hour mentally into six five-minute periods. The first half of the experiment is conducted in silence; in the second half, there is a degree of communication.

I ask them to spend the first five minutes silently contemplating what their lives will be like if their marriage does break up. Most people who plunge into divorce have no conception of the emotional shock and dislocation, the loneliness, the guilt feelings, and the sense of failure and purposelessness that all too often make up the price tag of this solution to their problems. Women are particularly vulnerable; time and time again I have had a wretchedly unhappy divorcee say to me: "If only I had known that it would be like this, if only I had known. . . ." Hindsight, they say, has 20-20 vision. But sometimes an imaginative forward-looking effort can be almost as good. Anyway, when two people sit silently together and contemplate the probable consequences of an act, they are establishing a certain rapport whether they know it or not.

In the second five minutes I ask them to stop judging their marriage partner and take a good look at themselves. I invite them to stand in each other's shoes for three hundred seconds and see themselves as the other sees them. This requires tremendous self-honesty, and in many cases such an effort becomes possible only because each feels that the other is making a similarly painful evaluation. But very often insight is gained into how much immaturity is involved on both sides. As one man said to me, "After five minutes of really looking at myself from Helen's point of view, that alarm clock's tick seemed awfully loud, and what it was saying was crystal clear. It was pointing out the basic flaw in my marriage, my preoccupation with *self, self, self, self!*"

In the third five minutes, I require them to think about the other lives that will be adversely affected by the termination of their marriage, especially the children who did not ask to be brought into a world in which they are callously deprived of one parent or the other. I have no patience with the familiar argument that a shaky marriage should be ended for the benefit of the children. A shaky marriage should be *repaired* for the benefit of the children! The fact that bickering and discord exist does not mean that the discord and bickering will always exist. It will cease if the marriage partners learn self-discipline and self-control, instead of rushing to get a divorce that may just enable them to repeat their old mistakes with some other individual.

In the fourth five minutes I ask that on alternate days each of them read aloud St. Paul's famous definition of love (I Corinthians 13:4-7). They are not to discuss or analyze it. They are simply to listen and meditate, especially on the emphasis given to *endurance* as an attribute of love.

In the fifth five minutes, I ask each of them to recall and

remind the other of some episode from the days when they were happy and in love, some moment of sharing or mutuality that no amount of bitterness can erase. There are many such mountain peaks in any marriage, and remembering them is a form of reliving them.

I know that if I were doing this myself, so many memories would come crowding in that it would be difficult to choose. The time in an English garden, during the depression years, when a terrifying sense of my own inadequacy as a minister swept over me and I told Ruth that I thought I was a miserable failure. And she told me to stop thinking about myself and to trust God. The blue-and-gold Sunday morning in Switzerland when our children decided to conduct services for us on the terrace of our chalet, the little white-covered table that they set up as an altar with a vase of wild flowers, the stupendous background of the Alps. The moment in the Holy Land when we stood before the tomb where Lazarus was raised from the dead, and felt for the first time the full impact of the power and truth of the Easter message. If Ruth and I had had a quarrel or any sort of difficulty, I think I would find it very hard to remember these things and not feel my heart flooded with love and gratitude, and a desperate desire to regain that former closeness. And other people have told me that this simple device has had a profound effect upon them, too.

In the last five minutes of this experiment designed to salvage a marriage on the rocks, I make the most significant and difficult demand: I ask each of the warring partners, speaking aloud, to tell the Author of the Universe, or whatever their concept of God may be, exactly what they think has gone wrong with their marriage and what their part in that failure has been. I ask them to summon up all their self-honesty and speak from the bottom of their hearts. And I promise them that if they will do this, they will find many of their difficulties melting away and a kind of compassion and tolerance flooding into them that will change their whole outlook and relationship to each other.

To carry out such an experiment calls for courage and self-discipline. It takes persistence, determination, control, all the qualities of mind and heart that add up to "stickability," which in a difficult situation is just about the most valuable human quality of all. But some people who tried it have told me that it saved their marriage.

I think the experiment works—when it works—because it succeeds in recasting the two people in the supportive role that is so essential to marriage. One of the greatest descriptive phrases in the Bible, referring to the love of God, tells us that "underneath are the everlasting arms." This image of God as the *supportive* force in the universe is profoundly comforting to me, and I think that marriage partners have to play a similar role; they have to *support* one another, not just in times of crisis but in the casual daily decisions and drudgeries, in the countless minor loyalties of thought and word and deed, that are part of a successful marriage. Living can be a solitary thing. It is only through mutual support that the essential loneliness of life can be overcome, and true closeness achieved.

The other day I heard a poignant story that will haunt me for a long time. A young mother left her small child unattended while she was doing the laundry in the basement. The child found some adult medicine, drank it all, and was dead on arrival at the hospital. The mother sat, stunned and stricken, waiting for her husband to come. What would he say? He idolized the child. When he did come, he took his wife in his arms and said just four words, over and over. "Darling," he said, "I love *you*." Nothing else, no questions, no recriminations, no blame. Just: "Darling, I love *you!*" He forgot about his own hurt and did his best to draw the protective cloak of his love around his suffering wife.

That man knew how to love. He was a supportive person. He was an inner-directed human being. There can be no higher goal, in this life, for us all.

MEMO TO THE READER NO. 5

Stop Staring at Stereotypes!

Sometimes, when I sit in my office trying to help people with their problems, it seems to me that very often when human relationships become badly tangled it's because the people involved are failing to deal with one another as *people*. They set up stereotypes in their minds, bleak images that fit their worst preconceptions. And if they stare at these stereotypes long enough, they become almost incapable of seeing anything else.

Not long ago, for example, an embattled husband was telling me about his mother-in-law. It seemed that his wife's father had died, and her elderly mother had come to live with them. This was his wife's idea, he told me fervently, not his. "I know it's my Christian duty," he said, "to regard everyone with charity—even my mother-in-law. But believe me, I find it easier to be fond of a man-eating shark!"

"Really?" I said. "What's wrong with her?"

"Well," he said. "Let's start with the beginning of the day. I used to get up early, fix my own breakfast peacefully, and go on off to work. But no more. My wife's mother likes to get up early too. She doesn't bother to get dressed, or comb her hair. She comes down looking like an underprivileged Gorgon in an old dressing gown and a pair of heelless slippers. When I hear her scuffing down the stairs, I lose all appetite for my breakfast."

"Is that all?" I asked him.

"No," he said. "That's just the beginning. She sits down at the table and then she scrunches up her toes. I can hear them popping inside those scuff slippers. Like firecrackers. Also, she has false teeth, and she clicks them. Like castanets. It's terrible!"

"She does sound a bit noisy," I admitted. "Anything else?"

"Yes," he said. "She reaches out a long, bony arm and pours herself some coffee. But she doesn't drink it like a

123

human being. She slurps it. Like a horse." Here he made a sound that did indeed resemble my recollections of equine gatherings around a watering trough that stood in a small Ohio town back in my early boyhood. "What," he demanded, "am I going to do?"

"If I tell you," I said, "will you do it?"

"Absolutely."

"Anything at all?"

"Anything at all!"

"Well, then, tomorrow morning, just before you leave for work, look back from the front door and say, 'Mother So-and-so, how about having lunch with me downtown today, just the two of us.' "

He looked at me as if I had six heads. "Are you kidding?"

"Not at all. Tell her you want to ask her advice about a gift you're planning to give your wife. Tell her you're going to take her to the best restaurant in town. And take her there too."

"What if she starts scrunching her toes and clicking her teeth? What if she . . ."

"She won't. She won't look like a Gorgon, either. She's a woman, isn't she? At least she was before she was a mother-in-law. Try it just for an hour, and see what happens."

Well, he did it. And he told me afterward that when she walked into the restaurant, he couldn't believe his eyes. She was well-dressed, well-mannered, pleasant, and intelligent. She discussed topics he had never heard her mention before. "And you know something," he concluded triumphantly, "since then she's started brushing her hair and getting dressed in the mornings!"

The point is, people want to be treated as people, not as stereotypes. Your husband isn't just your husband, he's also a man, with a man's need for importance and appreciation. And your wife isn't just your wife, she's also a woman, with a woman's need to be admired and protected and loved. My own mother once said to me, "Norman, you help a lot of people; why don't you help me? Why don't you stop treating me like a mother who's never supposed to be tired or discouraged or depressed and treat me like a human being who sometimes is?"

I never forgot that. And ever since, when I find myself typecasting a person as a "crashing bore" or a "frightful snob" or an "arrogant intellectual" or anything else, I try to make myself stop and see them as they really are: vulnerable, fallible, human mixtures of good and bad like myself . . . *people*.

Try it yourself, and you may be surprised sometimes at how your attitude changes. Now let's take a look at the area of life where there should be no stereotypes, where interpersonal attitudes are all-important: the family itself.

CHAPTER VII

The Family: Bedrock or Quicksand

The idea that the family is the cornerstone of society is as old as the written word. Two thousand years ago, Cicero said, "The seat of empire is at the fireside." He meant that the home is the place where discipline is taught, where character is formed, where the ideals that keep civilization going are passed from one generation to another.

If the family is strong, then the nation is strong. If the family is weak, the nation is weak. And what is the status of the family in America today? The word that comes to mind is "shaky."

Not all families, to be sure. But in general the symptoms of the moral revolution through which we are living can be seen plainly enough in family life. There is a breakdown of authority. There is a breakdown of discipline. There is a breakdown of communication. There is a breakdown of responsibility.

Now if the foundations on which a structure rests have become shaky, you must do one of two things: either tear the structure down, or fix the foundations. No attempt to abolish the family (various Communist regimes have tried it) has ever succeeded, and I feel sure that none ever will: the biological and spiritual factors are too strong. So that leaves us with a mighty job of foundation-fixing on our hands.

I remember one encouraging story of foundation-fixing that occurred a few years ago, right in Manhattan where I live. Down in the financial district, workmen were digging the excavation for a huge skyscraper—a sixty-story bank building—when they came upon some quicksand. The engineers were amazed, because most of the island of Manhattan is solid rock. But here was this quicksand which, as everyone knows, is hardly the ideal foundation for anything, let alone a sixty-story building.

They tried to pump it out. No good. They tried to fill it in.

No use. They summoned a learned professor of geology and asked him hopefully how long it would take that quicksand to turn into sandstone. About a million years, he said. More or less. This discouraged the bank board. They passed a resolution that they could not wait a million years; their depositors wouldn't like it.

Then someone suggested calling an outfit known as a chemical soil solidification company. When a representative appeared, they asked how long it would take them to change the quicksand into sandstone. "Well," said the man, "we're rather busy this week. But we can take care of it next week, if that's all right with you." Which was, you might say, an improvement on the original offer.

And they got the job. They drove up some trucks loaded with sodium silicate and calcium chloride, and they dumped these chemicals into the quicksand, and it turned into a substance strong enough to hold up a mighty skyscraper—and there it stands today.

Now what are the ingredients that can be mixed into a shaky family that will give it this sort of strength and durability? Is it possible to blend spiritual and emotional "chemicals" into a formula that will strengthen and sustain family relationships? I think it is, if the people who make up the family—especially the parents—will learn and accept the necessary disciplines. When family foundations are shaky, ninety-nine times out of a hundred it's because some of the members are neglecting the basic controls.

Technically speaking, neither my wife Ruth nor I qualify as child guidance experts. But we have brought up three youngsters who seem to have turned into well-integrated, outgoing, happy young adults. In the process, we worked out a handful of do's and don'ts that aided us tremendously in guiding these members of the next generation toward self-responsibility. A combination of love and discipline was our basic formula. All the suggestions I am about to offer reflect one or the other of these two main ingredients. And all require a degree of self-imposed control. Also our home was filled with faith and prayer; God for us was the chief cornerstone. This gave a warmth and a strength to our living, made us, in a very definite way, bigger and better than we might otherwise have been.

Since I have always believed that affirmatives are stronger and more useful than negatives, let's save the positive exhortations for last and begin with the don'ts. There are five of them. Here they are:

1. Don't give your children too many *things*. In our affluent and permissive society, this advice is very hard for most parents to follow. If fascinating toys and gadgets are available, if there is money to buy them, if the parent loves the child and wants to make it happy, then the pressure constantly to give things is enormous. And if there is on the part of the parent an uneasy feeling that he is not doing a very good job when it comes to child-raising, then a guilt factor may creep in which makes the gift-giving even more unreasonable and compulsive.

But the truth is, too many things do not lead to happiness, they lead to boredom. It was Thoreau, I think, who said that a man is rich in what he can do without. By the same paradox, a child can be very poor if his parents give him too much.

When children are given too many things too easily, several things happen—all of them bad. They lose, for one thing, the joy of anticipation, the almost unbearable pleasure-pain of waiting and hoping and wondering whether or not the long-sought object will ever arrive. I remember vividly, as a small boy in Ohio, going through this process. My brother and I longed for a bicycle—not one for each of us (that was beyond our wildest dreams), just one that we could both ride. In a small-town parson's family a bicycle represented a serious outlay of money. We were told that we might be able to have one some day, but that nobody knew when. So we waited. And hoped. And dreamed.

Months went by—in fact, I think it was years. But one day we were told that a bicycle was coming. Secondhand, to be sure, but a real, honest-to-goodness two-wheeler. I remember racing my brother down to the railroad station, quivering with anticipation. I remember how my heart pounded as the train rolled in. It's a wonder we didn't faint when the crate was finally unloaded. Excitement? What modern American child is likely to encounter such a thrill?

Another thing the gift-bombarded child may lose is his capacity for inventiveness. If diversions do not exist, normal children will invent them. In my childhood, boys spent untold hours fashioning scooters made of wood with skate wheels screwed to the bottom, and "racing-cars" made of wooden crates with small abandoned tricycle wheels. They were crude compared to modern toys, but we were proud of them. We made kites of newspapers pasted onto light wooden frames; they were homely looking things, but they flew. If we wanted something "store-bought," we usually had to earn the money for it by mowing lawns or delivering papers. Incidentally, this conviction that you had to work for what you got has stayed with most of us ever since.

My point is, there was a kind of built-in discipline in all this, a discipline that today's children no longer have. There are times when it seems to me that each modern invention carries an invisible price tag with it. Television, surely, is a great marvel; it has revolutionized communications. But does the child who becomes addicted to it ever really learn to read? Will he ever hunt for entertainment or enlightenment in a library when he can have distraction, as monotonous and predictable as chewing gum, simply by flipping a switch? I doubt it.

No one, certainly, is going to turn the clock back where these things are concerned. We lived in a materialistic society where enormous sums of money are spent every day by people who have a vested interest in wanting us to buy more of everything, more cars, more refrigerators, more gadgets, more toys. But a disciplined parent will be aware of the problem, and do what he can to minimize it. And someday his children will thank him.

2. Don't saddle them with your own fears, prejudices, or frustrations. This is a very common failing on the part of parents. I have had to deal with many cases of marital discord where the wife had been told by her mother that sex was sinful or disgusting, and consequently was unable to be a real wife. I have seen many men pushed into the wrong career by fathers who were trying to make their sons succeed where they failed. I have seen many mothers trying to compensate for their own lack of social success by turning their daughters into social butterflies. A frustrated actress-instinct displaced onto some hapless child is a familiar and frightening phenomenon in Hollywood, where almost anyone will tell you that all too often the mothers of child stars are insatiable in their thirst for vicarious recognition.

So if you have strong ambitions for your child, examine them carefully and make sure that they are not reflections of your own hidden desires. Many teachers have told me that the rise in classroom cheating is partly the result of intense parental pressure on the children to get good grades, no matter how. The current and curious tendency to push young girls into an absurd maturity long before it is right or natural —padded bras at ten, makeup at eleven, high heels at twelve —often is a displaced ambition on the part of the mother who hopes in some obscure way to be able to relive her own romantic years and can't wait for the process to begin. Just last week I had a letter from a bewildered thirteen-year-old who was upset because, going to meet her mother at a restaurant, she took along a girl friend. The mother, who was sitting with two women her own age, upbraided her daughter severely for appearing with a girl instead of a boy friend. Her tirade, apparently, was designed to impress her friends with the sexual precocity and desirability of her daughter—a twisted kind of ego-prop!

So it is well to remember that fear is contagious, that prejudice is contagious, indeed that all warped emotions are contagious, especially where impressionable children are concerned. So don't load your child with the emotional and psychological chains you have forged in your own life.

3. Don't be overprotective. Nothing retards maturity in a child more drastically than smother love. Ivy Baker Priest, former Treasurer of the United States, once told me that her father, who successfully raised a large family, used to say, "give every child a good big dose of neglect." Nothing stunts the capacity for self-realization quicker than a parent who refuses to let a child make any decisions, or even an occasional mistake. Mistakes can be good teachers.

Of course, if what a child proposes is foolish or dangerous, you have to say no. But I have noticed that where risky activities are concerned, the human body has a kind of wisdom of its own that applies the brakes when necessary. An adventurous child may climb a tree, tumble out, and break an arm—there is some risk inherent in anything. But the same child is not likely to turn somersaults on the edge of a precipice, or try to pet a rattlesnake. Indeed, you can argue that the overprotected child is more likely to be hurt than the less-sheltered one, because he hasn't learned by experience what he can do safely.

Overprotected children, constantly hearing "You can't do this" or "You mustn't do that" are likely to wind up with a first-class inferiority complex. After all, if the gods of their small world keep harping on their inadequacy, who are they to question it? And so, as they grow, self-doubt grows with them.

Sometimes a single negative or disparaging remark can do enormous damage to a person's belief in himself. I never forgot a story told me by the famous novelist, A. J. Cronin. He said that as a young medical student (he was a doctor before he was a writer), he had a professor of surgery who was harsh and outspoken and critical. One day this man stopped Cronin in the hall and told him that his performance was hopeless, that he might be an adequate general practitioner but that he would never be a surgeon. And Cronin believed him.

But then the young doctor went to a remote village in the Scottish highlands to practice. He was the only physician for miles around. One winter's day, with roads blocked by ice and snow, a tree fell on the son of the local pastor, crushing his spine and paralyzing him. Cronin knew that an operation was imperative; without it, the paralysis would be permanent. But he remembered what the professor said, and he was afraid to take the risk, because the slightest mistake could mean death for the boy.

The pastor himself urged Cronin to operate. He would pray for him, he said. God would help him. Cronin kept refusing. "All I could think of," he told me, "was the face of that man telling me that I could never be a surgeon."

But then something happened. I think, myself, that it was an answer to the pastor's prayers. But Cronin described it as a sudden surge of anger. "For the first time," he said, "I questioned the validity of that man's verdict. Who was he to tell me what I could or couldn't do? A kind of fury came over me and swept away the doubts and fears. I *knew* I could operate successfully. And with God's help I did!"

Confidence—that is one of the main pillars of self-responsibility. Without it, people are going to avoid responsibility because they doubt their own capacity to handle it.

As our children grew older, Ruth and I tried to give them more and more responsibility. Where money was concerned, for example, Ruth always gave them an allowance for all their major needs: clothes, travel, entertainment, and so on. If they mismanaged it, that was too bad; no more was forthcoming. Actually, none of the children handled money in the same way. Margaret was conservative, a saver. John was a lavish spender on things like books and phonograph records, often to the detriment of his appearance since he hated to "waste" money on clothes. Elizabeth was usually penniless long before her next "payday." But none of the children ever tried to wheedle more money out of us, and all are good money managers today.

Gauge your children's capacity for handling responsibility, give it to them, and keep hands off. There will be a few stubbed toes here and there, but write them off as growing pains. After all, nothing teaches self-control faster than a few well-learned mistakes!

4. Where discipline is concerned, don't vacillate. Nothing disturbs a child more than a parent who is stern one minute and permissive the next. They want fair rules, but they also want consistency in the application of those rules. If the rules seem to change from day to day, who can blame them for becoming resentful and confused?

My psychiatrist friend, Smiley Blanton, who specialized in child guidance for years, has just one rule for parents in this area: "Never give a child an unnecessary order," he says, "but when you do give one, make it stick!"

Too many of us parents, I think, have become addicted to the partial or conditional "No." "If you must smoke," we say wistfully to our teenagers, "I'd prefer that you do it at home." What kind of guidance is that? Why don't we say to them forthrightly, "While you are underage, I am responsible for your health as well as your conduct. Smoking has been proven scientifically to be extremely bad for you. Therefore I tell you not to smoke!"

Would they rebel—and do it anyway? Possibly. But probably not. Children respect clearness and firmness. They want desperately to hitch their allegiance to something solid. Who can blame them for being dismayed if they find the hitching post wandering all over the corral?

5. Don't stifle their talent for religion. This may seem a strange phase, but I believe children have an instinctive capacity for faith, a simplicity that makes it easy for them to believe in God, a sensitivity to the role of love in human affairs, which, after all, is the basic teaching of Christianity. But often these attributes are weakened or wiped out altogether by parents who make religion a lifeless or forbidding thing, or even something to be avoided altogether.

How can you help them keep a talent for religion? You must first believe, yourself, that religion is worth having, and act and live as if it were. In this area, above all others, it is

fatal to say to a child "Do as I say—not as I do." But there
are also many *little* things you can do.

When you talk about God, make it sound as if He were a
friend and companion and helper, which He is, not some awful Recorder of Trangressions bent on revenge or punishment.

If you pray together, don't bore the children with long,
archaic prayers endlessly repeated. Make them short, intense
conversations with God. Pray about the problems that children
have, not just your own. Try to make them see that prayer
is not just an empty or meaningless recitation of things that
God knows already, but as Emerson said, "a way of looking
at things from the highest possible point of view."

Say grace at mealtime, but take turns saying it, and let
each member of the family talk to God in his own way. Traditional graces are often melodious and beautiful, but to a
child they can also become very monotonous and meaningless.

Learn some of the old hymns and sing them together . . .
Sunday nights before supper is a good time. You'll be surprised at how lively some of them are. It was Martin Luther,
wasn't it, who said he didn't see why the Devil should have
all the good tunes? Well, the Devil doesn't!

If the children are in the bedtime-story age, tell some
of the old Bible stories, using your own words. The Bible is
full of great clanging battle stories, tender love stories, cliff-
hangers like Daniel in the lion's den or Jonah and the whale,
cataclysms like the Red Sea swallowing up Pharaoh's armies,
or the walls of Jericho tumbling down. Those stories haven't
endured two thousand years for nothing. I have a modernized
version of the battle between David and Goliath that I use
occasionally in a sermon if I think the congregation is dozing.
It's the classic story of the underdog who whips the arrogant
bully—and it never fails to wake them right up! Stories like
these help children absorb a faith that helps them make
valid moral decisions as free men later on.

Try to make religion a natural part of living, like eating or
breathing. Try to make the children see that while it can be
demanding, it need not be gloomy or pious or dull. The Bible
is not a gloomy book, nor does it recommend gloom. On the
contrary, "Rejoice . . ." it says, "and again I say, Rejoice!"

In fact the three great words of the New Testament are joy
—joy—joy. Jesus said, "These things have I spoken unto you,
that my joy might remain in you, and that your joy might
be full." Christianity began with singing over the plains of

Bethlehem and the New Testament ends with a great multitude whom no man can number. And they were singing. And all through the New Testament there is singing—singing in pain, singing in adversity, singing even in death. As an ancient writer said, "There is in Christianity something akin to the song of the skylark and the babbling of brooks."

One more thing: I believe a parent should pray for his children and let them know that he does. Prayer of this kind, I'm convinced, forms a kind of invisible envelope of love that surrounds them wherever they go, and if they are at all sensitive they will feel its comforting presence. It may also, at times, deter them from doing something foolish or unwise or unethical. It's hard deliberately to disappoint someone who tells you that he makes a habit of praying for you. If you don't believe this, try it some time!

So much for the five deadly don'ts. Now here are some not-so-deadly do's.

1. The first, and simplest, is this: *show affection*. Children live in an expanding world full of problems and trials. They need assurance to cope with these problems and face up to these trials, and the deepest assurance in their lives comes from the knowledge that they can count on their parents' love.

Not their parents' approval always: they can and do sometimes forfeit this temporarily. But love is, or should be, their birthright—even more than food and shelter and protection. They are entitled to it, and they need to be reminded that it is always there. If my children have been separated from me for a while, and they call long-distance, I try to end the conversation with a cheerful, "Remember, we all love you!" They know we do, but they like to be reminded, and the reminder itself strengthens the underlying truth.

Affection can be expressed in many ways, in a shared joke, a word, a glance, a touch. Small babies need to be cuddled and petted; if they are totally deprived of this, they become neurotic. We never fully outgrow this need for touchingness, although it is probably the first bond to disappear when things are going badly between people. A juvenile judge told a friend of mine that he had presided over hundreds of cases involving juvenile delinquents and their parents, but that never once, as father and son stood before the bench, had he seen the father put his hand on his son's shoulder, or touch or attempt to reassure him in any way. This is a sad thing.

So let your love for your children be constantly demonstrated. Train yourself to express it as often as you can, and you'll be surprised to see how much is reflected right back to you.

2. *Trust them.* In our family we found that nothing develops a sense of responsibility in children more swiftly and surely than the knowledge that their parents believe that they will do the right thing. This is one more illustration of the enormous power of faith. If you expect a person to try to take advantage of you, you are creating a climate in which unpleasant things are much more likely to happen than if you trust him and let him know that you trust him.

Where children are concerned, parents have to scold and correct and say no so much that it is easy for the children to begin to wonder if they are loved and trusted after all. And if they feel they are not trusted, then half their motivation for good behavior is gone. After all, something in them whispers, if these people expect the worst, why not give it to them?

I was a guest one day on Art Linkletter's television program in Hollywood and was answering questions from the studio audience. Some question came up about trusting children and I happened to speak of my daughter Elizabeth, at the time a student at Mount Holyoke College. I stated that I absolutely trusted her to do the right and wise thing at all times, that my confidence in her was full and complete in everything.

I forgot that this program would be heard nationwide, including Mount Holyoke College, and when I returned home, Elizabeth telephoned me, "I hear you told the whole country you trust me." When I started to apologize for publicizing my trust so widely, she said softly, "You can, for Mommy and you have always made me feel you believe in me."

And I was very touched the next time I went to the college when one of her classmates said with sincerity, "You're right, Dr. Peale. She is trustworthy."

A friend of mine named Floyd Starr runs a school for boys who have been in trouble with the law. Floyd is convinced that there is no such thing as a naturally "bad" boy. If a boy behaves badly, he says, it is because he has been treated badly somewhere along the line, by life, or by his parents, or by something.

Floyd told me once of driving into town with one of his boys who was sullen, withdrawn, difficult to reach. When they got to their destination, Floyd took ten dollars from his pocket and handed it to the youngster. "I'll be busy for an hour or so," he said. "Get yourself some lunch and bring me the change. And here are the keys to the car, in case you need it."

The boy looked at him incredulously. "Have you forgotten what I was arrested for, Mr. Starr? It was car-stealing."

"I know," said Starr. "But that's all behind you now. I believe in you. I trust you."

The boy's eyes filled with tears. "Oh," he said brokenly, "why didn't my father or mother ever say that?"

Why not, indeed? After all, does it take so much willpower or self-discipline to say "I love you" or "I trust you" occasionally to a child? Apparently, sometimes, it does.

3. Encourage them to think for themselves. Most parents are probably convinced that they do a good job in this area. But I have often noticed that if children try to think for themselves, and if their opinions differ from their parents' opinion, it sometimes causes great alarm and despondency on the part of the older generation.

Writing recently in a scientific journal, Brock Chisholm makes this point bluntly. "Unfortunately," he writes, "very large numbers of people all over the world have been specifically taught in childhood not to think, because thinking would lead to questioning the certainties of the elders, and this has not been allowed in most cultures."

This is all wrong. Sooner or later adolescents must break away from their parents, form their own ideas, stand on their own feet. And if the opinions they form seem startling or radical—well, if a youngster isn't a bit of a firebrand at twenty he is likely to be a stuffed shirt at forty. "How's your boy doing at college," someone asked a bishop. "Fine, fine," said the bishop. "He's an atheist just now." That bishop was a wise and perceptive parent. And I imagine the two of them had some lively and stimulating conversations, too!

I remember Dr. Ernest Scott, a saintly professor of the New Testament in Union Theological Seminary. He was the gentlest of Christians and most proper, so I was startled but very impressed when I heard him say: "A boy who is not a socialist by twenty is a fool and who is not over it by twenty-five is a damned fool."

One way to encourage children to think for themselves is to discuss actual life situations at the dinner table and ask the children to express their opinions or reactions. At one point, when I was conducting a question-and-answer page for a national magazine, we were getting a flood of letters from people with all sorts of ethical problems and dilemmas. Very often, in selecting questions to be answered, I'd bring the letters home, read them aloud at the supper table, and ask Margaret, John, and Elizabeth for their comments. It was surprising how seriously they took these discussions, how vehemently they argued among themselves, and how sound their verdicts usually were.

Any parent can do this, and actually it can be a lot of fun. Here are a few typical life situations in which the moral issue involved will stretch young minds . . . or for that matter old ones.

A man is killed in a fall on his apartment stairs, leaving a wife and two children penniless. The superintendent had reported the faulty stairs to the owner of the apartment, who had done nothing about them. The superintendent's wife feels that she should tell the widow, who could then sue the landlord. But the owner gave the superintendent, an alcoholic, his job, and the wife is grateful. What should she do?

A man who has been dismissed from his job for stealing is unable to get other work in town. He convinces a friend of his that he is sorry and has reformed. He then asks the friend to write a letter of recommendation for an out-of-town job. But he doesn't want him to mention the stealing episode. Should the friend write such a letter, or not?

At a family dinner one night, a schoolteacher admits that she has Communist friends and is sympathetic to some of their views, although she is not a member of the Communist Party. Her cousin, who was at the dinner, is confused. Should she report her cousin to the school board? To the F.B.I.? Should she merely try to change her point of view? What should she do?

A man released as cured after two years in a mental institution is refused employment when he tells the truth about the nature of his illness. If he doesn't find work soon, his family will have to go on relief. The wife is urging her husband to write on his job application that he has been working for her brother. The brother will confirm this falsehood if necessary. What should the man do?

A woman develops a serious heart condition which means that she may die suddenly at any time, and at best has only a few months to live. The doctor stresses her need for peace of mind. But she has said more than once that she hopes she will be given enough warning to prepare her children for her death and make her peace with God. Should her husband tell her the medical facts, or not?

A man's wife has been confined in a mental institution for five years. The doctors say her case is virtually hopeless. The man, who has two small children, meets and falls in love with a woman who would make a good wife and mother. Should he end his first marriage and remarry, or remain true to his marriage vows?

Life is full of such dilemmas, and children are going to encounter them sooner or later. If now and then you bring them up at the dinner table, and work out a solution that amounts to a family verdict, you'll find that the invisible ties that hold the family together are somehow strengthened, and that it's a rewarding experience for all concerned.

4. Cultivate the ability to communicate with them. This is not always easy; children can and often do retreat into an aloofness that shuts out the adult world. But you have to break through this aloofness if you are to teach the child what he needs to know.

With small children, one of the easiest ways to break through is with a story. The old McGuffey readers that were used for so many years in American schools were full of stories, some dramatic, some patriotic, some frankly designed to get across a moral point. They were highly successful, too. I'm not sure that we should ever have abandoned them.

As a matter of fact, a story is the best way to get across a point to anybody—not just a child. The parables of Jesus were the greatest short-shorts ever told: He made His listeners see and feel and hear what was going on without wasting a word. "A certain man went down from Jerusalem to Jericho, and fell among thieves. . . ." Instantly you know who, what, and where . . . and you also want to know what happened next. The moral impact of this parable about the Good Samaritan—that inner-directed man!—comes at the end.

If a story points up the need for self-discipline or self-control, as many of the parables do, so much the better. One of the most effective modern stories along these lines that I ever read was called "To Kill a Devil." It was about a man who went down to South Africa in the gold rush days and made a fortune in gold mining. In the beginning he was disciplined and tough, but after he got rich he became soft and easygoing.

One day, when he was inspecting one of his mines, there was a cave-in. His companions escaped, but this man was no longer able to move quickly. He was trapped, all alone, deep in the earth. Tons of rock filled the corridor; he lay in a little space no wider than a coffin. There he stayed, hour after hour, in the total darkness, fighting claustrophobia, sometimes screaming with fear.

Eventually rescuers got to him and dug him out. He was physically unharmed, but that night when he went to bed, terror seized him. Every time he closed his eyes he felt himself back in his hideous underground tomb; he could hear himself screaming.

But while this man's body had turned soft, his spirit had not. At about midnight he got up, had his horse saddled, and rode to the mine. He had himself lowered to the same level where the disaster had occurred. He sent everyone back to the surface. Then he blew out the light he had with him and forced himself to sit there in the same place, in the same darkness, until he conquered his fears.

It was sunup when he finally rode back into town. "Where have you been?" asked an astonished friend who saw him. "To kill a devil," the man replied. It was the devil of fear, and he *had* killed it . . . by self-discipline, by self-control.

Often it seems to me that when parents fail to communicate with their older children it is because they are treating them as possessions rather than as people. We are not inclined to communicate with our possessions! But children are not outright gifts from life, they are only on loan to us for a number of years. And so, when a child reaches the age of reason, it is foolish to make communication a one-way street, to give him arbitrary orders and say, in effect, "Do thus and so because I tell you," or "Be good because I say so."

As children, my brothers and I were lucky, because this was never my father's way. "Well," he'd say, "let's talk this thing over—let's look at it from all points of view and see if we can't make sense out of it." And usually we could. The only really fierce "don't" that he gave us was "don't lie. Tell the truth, and I'll try to help you, no matter how bad the trouble is. But don't lie!"

I believe it was the ancient Persians whose educational system consisted of teaching a boy just two things: to ride a horse and tell the truth. Those are two pretty basic forms of discipline, when you come right down to it. But to be a truth-teller a child must be able to communicate easily, and he will be able to do this only if he has faith in his parents' love for him and in their sense of justice.

So try to keep the family lines of communication open at all times and at all cost. No effort that you can make will pay better dividends.

3. Show them what self-discipline is. In the final analysis, the best way for a parent to teach any virtue is to exhibit it in his own life. The best sermon is a good example, because it is wordless and therefore doesn't arouse the antagonism that the voice of authority often does.

Self-control is not just a matter of facing great crises successfully; it's also a matter of enduring the frictions and annoyances of day-to-day living. Imagine, for example, a simple household scene: a windy day in March, a clothesline in the back yard, a hard-working housewife hanging out Monday's wash while her small children in galoshes play happily on the muddy turf. The last garment is being pinned to the heavily loaded line. A gust of March wind sweeps around the corner of the house. The clothes flap wildly, the strain is too great, the line breaks—and a whole week's wash-ing lands in the mud!

Now watch that mother's face—as you may be sure the children are watching it—to see how she will react to this domestic disaster. Exasperation? Certainly. But then what? An outburst of futile rage? Tears? A few ill-chosen words? Or will she somehow manage to force a smile, turn the episode into a wry joke played on Mommy by the prankish wind, call the kids good-humoredly to help her salvage what she can? Control or non-control, that is the issue. Either way, she is going to leave a mark on her children's impressionable minds. And incidentally, her victory or defeat in this small, intense, unsung battle with herself will also affect her ability to meet and deal with future crises, large or small.

Calmness, steadiness, control . . . these attributes impress young people greatly, because they are usually so volatile themselves. A friend of mine told me once that his father's ability to withstand disappointment or frustration always filled him with pride and admiration. He added that once he had asked his father how he maintained such serenity. "Well," said the older man with a smile, "on such occasions, instead of flying into a great rage, I try to fly into a great calm!"

Fly into a great calm—I never forgot that phrase. In fact, I have tried ever since—not always successfully, I fear— to live by it.

Self-discipline on the part of parents can take many forms. For example, if a parent will control his anger with a child, even when the anger is justified, the child may remember the control long after any outburst or any punishment would be forgotten. In my college days at Ohio Wesleyan I had a classmate who was expelled for a flagrant violation of college rules. He had to go home and tell his father what had happened. And he dreaded this confrontation more than anything that had ever happened in his young life. He sat in the hall, he told me later, waiting for his father to come home. His stomach was tied in knots. Finally the door opened and his father came in. He saw the boy and looked surprised. "Why aren't you in school?" he asked.

The boy took a deep breath and said that he had been expelled.

The father stood quietly. "Why?"

The boy told him why.

The father hung his hat on the old-fashioned hatrack in the corner of the hall. "Well," he said, "they were right. You should have been expelled. Now we'll have to make some other plans. Let's go and have supper and talk about them."

That father was wise enough to know that his son was already suffering the consequences of his misdeeds, that recriminations would not make things any better, that the future was more important than the past. He was strong enough to control his own feelings of hurt and disappointment. And his son never forgot it. He went on to another college and never made such a mistake again.

I have always thought that the Bible is right: the sins of the father are passed on to succeeding generations. But this is only half the story. The virtues of the fathers can be passed along, too. If a father is an honest and upright man, and if he establishes any sort of adequate relationship with his son or sons, it is going to be very hard for those boys to run off the track. The desire to emulate and imitate is too strong.

Once, I remember, I was asked to preach in the chapel at Bucknell University. When my train arrived, very early in the morning, I was met by a cheerful young student who told me that the president of the college was away, and that he had been designated to act as my guide and companion during my short stay. He drove me to a fraternity house. It was so early that no one was in the dining room, but he sat me down and brought me a fine breakfast. "That was really good," I said when I finished. "You're an expert waiter. But maybe I should also thank the cook."

"Why, sure," he said and led me into the kitchen. There he put a white chef's cap on his head. "To tell you the truth," he said, "I'm also the cook."

Well, my guide-waiter-cook-chauffeur finally took me to the chapel. In the service that preceded my sermon, a splendid college choir sang, and one soloist was particularly impressive. I turned to look at him. It was my friend again!

Afterward, when he drove me back to the train, I complimented him on his extraordinary energy, and range of activities. "Tell me," I said, "have you always been like this?"

"No," he said. "A couple of years ago I was about as spoiled and useless a kid as you could imagine. We had money and lived well, and I took it all for granted. Then one night my father came home and told us that there had been some sort of financial disaster and that we were broke. He wasn't panicky, and he didn't blame anyone else. He just said that he was going to have to start all over again, and that things would be tough for a while . . . no luxuries, no free rides to college or anywhere else. Well, when I saw my father standing there, taking adversity like that, something seemed to happen inside of me, and I said to myself, 'From now on, boy, you're going to act like this man's son!' I decided to work my way through college, and I came up here to Bucknell and . . . and here I am!"

You see how, inside a family that is really a family, the spark of determination that lights the fires of civilization can be handed on!

I remember another episode where paternal self-control made an indelible impression on a young man. This story was told me by Charles Edison, son of the great inventor, Thomas A. Edison. On the night of December 9, 1914, when Charles was in his twenties, the huge Edison industrial plant in West Orange, N.J., was destroyed by fire. The loss was estimated at two million dollars. The owners were insured for only about a tenth of that amount, due to the mistaken notion then prevalent that concrete buildings were completely fireproof.

The old inventor at that time was sixty-seven, and most men would have been crushed by such a disaster. But his son told me that at the height of the fire, his white-haired father clutched him by the shoulder and shouted enthusiastically in his ear, "Find your mother and bring her down here. She'll never see such a magnificent sight as long as she lives!" Later he said earnestly to Charles, "There is great value in a catastrophe like this. All our mistakes have been burned up. Now we can start all over again!" And within ten weeks the Edison company was back in full production.

I thought of this noble legacy of optimism and self-control the other day when I was in California. But what a contrast! At the place where we were staying there was a swimming pool. The lifeguard was a tall, blond boy, well-built and handsome. But I never met a more mixed-up kid in my life. We had several talks, and he told me a lot about himself. His parents were divorced. His mother took a lover, brought this man home, and lived openly with him. Soon his mother's younger sister came to stay in the house. She had a husband somewhere, but this did not deter her from seducing her nephew—then a youngster of sixteen. "It's really a rotten world, isn't it?" he said to me. "I don't care whether I do well or badly in it. I guess I don't care about anything." In a way, that boy was dead—dead at nineteen—and it's not too farfetched to say that his own parents murdered him.

The cornerstone of that home had not only cracked, it had rotted. I first let the boy see that I cared for him and respected him as a person. I told him all the stories I knew of boys who had risen above such families. I told him of a friend of mine whose father, a real drunk, had been killed while driving on a lonely road with a woman, a notorious local tramp. The car in which they were riding hit a bridge abutment and both were sprawled dead in a ditch. This son gave up every personal hope and went to work, not only to support his mother and two younger sisters but, as he put it, to wipe clean the family name. It wasn't easy, but he did it and the family is now perhaps the most highly respected in that community.

The boy at the swimming pool kept telling me what a "lousy world" it is and how "dirty" he felt himself to be. I was able to put him in touch with some young people his own age who had found an exciting life-changing experience. They were extremely modern, sophisticated young people who had found spiritual answers that not only satisfied but made them extremely happy. We exposed this spirit-dulled young fellow to the contagion of these youngsters, and the same power of Christ that had reached them got through to him. "Old things are passed away; behold, all things are become new" for him. In fact he later used these New Testament words to describe the amazing change that came over him. "I'm living in a different world, a wonderful, clean, and happy world. I wouldn't have believed it possible."

That, perhaps, was an extreme case. But here on my desk as I write is a letter from a sixteen-year-old high school girl in Cincinnati who was arrested for shoplifting. She asks me, rather pathetically, why I think she stole things. "There was no reason at all," she writes. "Our family is well-to-do. I have plenty of spending money."

No reason at all? Elsewhere in her letter is this paragraph: "Ever since my sister and I have been old enough to walk, our parents have made us go to church. We had no choice in the matter. Sometimes we'd go somewhere else and tell our parents we had been to church. They never knew the difference, because they were never there themselves."

No reason at all? Of course there was a reason, even if it was an unconscious one. It was to pay her parents back for their injustice and hypocrisy, their do-as-I-say-not-as-I-do methods of raising a family. She wanted to humiliate and embarrass them, and she did.

Such motivation lies behind a great deal of anti-social behavior. In fact, one psychiatrist I know often asks his patients, "Whom are you acting *against?* Whom are you shoplifting *against*, or getting drunk *against*, or committing adultery *against?*" It's a good question for parents to ask themselves if their children's performance is consistently bad: whom are they acting against—and why?

Not long ago the Houston, Texas, Police Department issued a grim little set of rules for parents who really want to turn their children into delinquents. Here they are:

Give the child everything he wants so he will grow up believing the world owes him a living. When he picks up bad words, laugh at him and tell him he is cute. Let him read any printed matter he can get his hands on; be careful that his drinking glasses are sterilized but let his mind feed on garbage. Quarrel frequently in the presence of your children so they will not be too shocked when the home is broken up later. Give a child all the spending money he wants and never let him earn his own. Take his part against neighbors, teachers and policemen on the grounds that they are all prejudiced against your child.

What are the Texas policemen really saying? They are the guardians of law, the symbols of external authority. And yet they are saying exactly what I have been trying to say in this chapter: that there must be inner controls if civilization is to endure, that these inner controls must be taught by disciplined parents in the home, that only thus can a nation produce people strong enough to face the challenge of the destructive forces of the universe.

"Train up a child," says the Bible, "in the way he should go: and when he is old, he will not depart from it."

What a responsibility—and what an opportunity!

MEMO TO THE READER NO. 6

The Springboard of Optimism

"Well," you might say to me at this point, "you've been talking for more than half a book now about the need for self-discipline, self-control, inner-directedness and all that. But how, specifically, do you acquire these things? How do you even begin?"

You start the way all journeys start, with a single step. Only in this case it's not a physical step, it's a mental one: *You have to decide that you can do it.* You have to believe that you can accomplish the journey. You have to visualize yourself leaving Point A and arriving at Point B. You have to push all your doubts and hesitancies aside, set the compass of your willpower on the goal and keep it there, day after day, week after week, month after month if necessary.

Once you do this, *really* do it, the chances of failure diminish almost to zero. You're like a high-powered automobile that has shifted from neutral into high gear. A great psychiatrist once said, "The basic factor in physics is force; the basic factor in human affairs is the realizable wish." That's what you have to do: you have to seize upon a realizable wish and hang on until it becomes a reality.

Once you take this all-important first step, you stop being an "if" person and become a "how" person. An "if" person is forever listening to his fears. He begins every thought with a wince. "If only I knew how to cope with this thing . . ." "If only I had done this instead of that . . ." "If I just had better luck . . ." "If nothing goes wrong, maybe I can do it . . ." Nobody gets very far by being an "if" thinker. "If" thinking magnifies obstacles; it's full of fear, resentment, confusion and inertia.

A "how" thinker, on the other hand, sweeps all the ifs out of the way. He thinks: "Here's a situation; how can I improve it?" Or, "Here's a problem; how can I lick it?" Or, "There's the goal I've set for myself; how do I get to it?" The "how" thinker doesn't drain energy out of himself by asking *if;* he puts dynamism into himself by asking *how?*

Now what is the key quality that distinguishes a "how" thinker from an "if" thinker? It's optimism, isn't it? It's the belief that most things are going to turn out right, not wrong. It's faith-plus-imagination-plus-enthusiasm. It's a springboard that can send you soaring through life. Just about every successful person I know is full of it.

I remember meeting three different people on three successive days some years ago who were so full of this shining characteristic that I've never forgotten them. Optimism is contagious, and after leaving each of these individuals I felt like a storage battery that had been plugged into a giant dynamo.

The first was a man I met at a machinery manufacturers' convention. What I know about machinery would rattle around in a thimble, but these men asked me to give them a talk, and I did. Actually, I got much more than I gave, because at dinner I sat next to this man who manufactured giant roadbuilding machines and was absolutely thrilled by his work. He talked about his mechanical monsters as if they were his children. He praised their strength, their durability, their versatility. "There is nothing more wonderful," he said, "than the astounding machines that American business is ordering from science and that science is delivering to American business." He pounded the table in his enthusiasm as he assured me that there was no limit to what a machine could be made to do, if directed by a first-class mind, and I got almost as excited as he was.

The next night I attended a banquet in Mansfield, Ohio. There I sat beside a man who was not only a great novelist but a great farmer. His name was Louis Bromfield. He was a genius with words, but he was also a genius with soil. He lived and wrote near Mansfield at a place called Malabar Farm. I said to him, "I understand, Mr. Bromfield, that you have done some great things with worn-out soil."

He smiled at that. He had a seamed, wind-chiseled face and a tall, rangy body that looked as if it would have been more at home on a tractor than behind a typewriter. "There's no such thing as worn-out soil," he told me. "Man mistreats the soil; he robs it of its chemical elements of fertility. But if you know how to restore those elements by means of scientific agriculture, there's no limit to what you can do with the soil." He talked on and on, with passionate eloquence, and I was spellbound. Here was another optimist, another enthusiast.

The third optimist, the one I met the next day, wasn't there in the flesh at all, but he was certainly there in the spirit. I was in New Jersey to be present at the ceremonial opening of an old-fashioned rolltop desk that had belonged to Thomas A. Edison. When Edison died, his desk was closed and locked. Now it was to be opened on the hundredth anniversary of his birth. And so at the given hour, exactly one hundred years after the great inventor was born, they opened the desk and found everything as he had left it, with notes and plans for future experiments . . . he was always looking forward, never back. And as we sat around talking, some one recalled two things Edison had said. "Science has barely scratched the surface of the possibilities in the universe," he said. And he added, "There's no limit to what you can do with non-human nature."

No limit—that's the optimist's phrase. No limit to what you can do with a machine, no limit to what you can do with the soil, no limit to what you can do with non-human nature. Well, if there's no limit to the possibilities in those realms, there certainly is no limit to what human beings, with God's help, can do to improve and strengthen themselves.

There's one area where I think most of us could do a lot *right now* to improve and strengthen ourselves, and that's in the realm of physical fitness, the way we use—or abuse—our own bodies. All too often the marvelous envelope that houses our souls or spirits gets less care than we give—say—the family car. But self-discipline in matters of health can pay marvelous dividends, too. In the next chapter, I'll tell you how this realization was brought home to me—and why I think it's important to you.

CHAPTER VIII

The Challenge of Our Physical Selves

Some years ago, my wife and I spent a winter week-end with some friends—call them Martha and Henry—at their seaside cottage on one of the Carolina beaches. Henry was a tall, lean man in his late fifties, editor of a fair-sized newspaper in a neighboring town. I had always admired him for his tremendous mental energy; it crackled in the editorials that he wrote and in the dynamic way he talked. He is one of the most alive people I know.

The first morning was bright and cold. "Let's go for a walk," he suggested. I like walking on a windswept beach, so off we went. We hadn't gone far before we came to a great piece of timber left by the tide. My friend surveyed it with delight. "Now, there," he said, rubbing his hands with satisfaction, "is a marvelous piece of wood. We must have it."

"Have it?" I echoed. "Why, that thing must weigh two hundred pounds!"

"That's all right," he said. "We'll saw it in half. Come on! We'll get a saw."

We got the saw. I watched him cut the timber in half. We carried one half back to the cottage. When we finally dropped it, I nearly dropped with it. I sat down on the sea wall and huffed and puffed. "Let's wait a minute," I said plaintively, "before we get the other half."

"Oh," he said, "I'll get it. You stay here and catch your breath."

I watched him walk down the beach, drag the plank to a vertical position, and tilt it onto one shoulder. He came back, walking slowly but confidently, the timber making a huge T against the sparkling ocean. At the sea wall he gave a shrug, dropped it with a crash, and dusted the sand off his hands. "There!" he said with satisfaction.

I knew this man was no show-off. "Henry," I said, "what do you think you're doing? Aren't you afraid of breaking

149

your back or straining your heart or something? You don't need those pieces of wood. What's the idea?"

He laughed and sat down beside me. "Norman," he said, "you may know a lot about the human soul and the human mind, but apparently you don't know much about the human body. Oh, I've heard you say that it's a marvelous machine, and in a limited sense it is. But there's one tremendous difference. A machine doesn't care whether it works or not. The human body does. It's designed for work, it needs work, it's hungry for work. Sure, it's going to wear out eventually, but the notion that physical activity hastens that day is all wrong. Hard, steady use retards that day." He slapped me on the shoulder. "Come on; let's walk!"

We set off down the beach, and my friend kept on talking. "There are tremendous rewards," he said, "in disciplining your body, in assigning it tasks that make it work. You burn up aggression and frustration. You sleep better and eat better and think better. Of course I didn't need those two planks. And left to itself, my body wouldn't undertake the labor of hauling them home either. The mind has to tell the body what to do, and the will has to make it do it. An expert on race horses told me once that the greatest thoroughbred in the world would be useless in a race without a trainer to condition him and a jockey on his back to hold him in when necessary and urge him on at the right moment. Well, your body is like the horse and your mind is the trainer and your will is the jockey. They have to work together if you're going to run a good race in this life. How is your mind going to be clear and alert if the body that houses it is only half alive? How is your body going to be the superb machine it's designed to be unless your mind and will control and direct it?"

"*Mens sana in corpore sano*," I murmured, using one of the few Latin tags I know.

"A healthy mind in a healthy body. Exactly," he said. "The Greeks and the Romans were more aware of the connection than we are. They knew there had to be a body-mind balance if a person hoped to achieve self-fulfillment. And it was easier for them, really, than it is for us. They had to use their muscles. We use machines. Automobiles have just about atrophied our leg muscles. We spend most of our lives sitting at desks, or in front of television sets. Most of us eat more food than we burn up, and it turns to fat. Most of us do our best to dodge any form of physical exertion. Many of us fill our lungs with tobacco smoke—a proven killer. Many of us seem to be incapable of enjoying a social function without loading our bloodstreams with alcohol—a toxic depressant. We take these amazing, God-given bodies of ours which, if cared for, can do simply astonishing things, and what do we do? We beat them, literally, to death!" He looked at me speculatively. "How long is it since you've pushed your body anywhere near its capacity for physical work?"

"Well," I said defensively, "quite a while, I guess. But I keep busy trying to think up sermons and talking to people around the country. . . ."

"I know, I know," he said impatiently. "You're always urging people to live fully and boldly. And that's fine. But most of what you say deals with mental and moral attitudes only."

"I don't think you have to be in top physical condition to be in good moral condition," I said.

"It may not be essential," my friend said. "But it certainly helps." We had come to a place where a little tidal river coiled into the sea. We stood and watched the placid water flow past. "I'll tell you how I know it helps," he said suddenly. "This is a story I've never told to anyone. It happened a long time ago, when I was a lot younger, and it happened right here at the beach. Martha took the kids away to the mountains for a month, so I was a summer bachelor. And about midway through that month I met a girl, a beautiful girl looking for excitement. She made it clear that I had a green light where she was concerned. All I had to do was say when and where.

"In those days, as an ambitious young newspaperman, I smoked a lot and drank more than was good for me. As for exercise, I figured I could take it or leave it. If I was getting a bit soft and flabby—and I was—it didn't seem to matter, because most of my friends were too. We were like those people in that book by Aldous Huxley, *Brave New World*, whose motto was, 'Never put off till tomorrow the fun you can have today.' And so one week-end I put my conscience in mothballs and arranged a meeting with her for Saturday night.

"I woke up early Saturday morning with a bit of a hangover; I'd played poker until late the night before. I decided to get up, put on my swimming trunks, and take a walk on the beach to clear my head. I took an ax along, because the wreck of an old barge had come ashore down the beach, and there was a lot of tangled rope that was worth salvaging. No one else was on the beach. Everything was calm and opalescent and still.

"I came to the old barge and cut away some of the rope. And there was something about the freshness of the morning and the feel of the ax that made me want to keep on swinging it. So I began to chop in earnest, right down through the hull of the wreck. I got tired almost at once, but I thought that if I kept on I'd get a second wind, and I did.

"Now, there's something almost hypnotic about the rhythm of chopping wood. The ax head flashes in the sun, and the chips go flying as the blade bites in, and you feel the shock all the way through your wrists and up your arms and into your shoulders. And you begin to perspire, and the sweat seems to lubricate your muscles and clear your brain, and your mind decides where you want the ax to go and your reflexes put it there, and your breathing becomes synchronized, and the whole marvelous creation that is *you* begins to function on a new level of rightness—it's in harmony with life, or living, or the pulse of the universe, or something.

"Well, as I kept on chopping, a strange thing began to happen. I felt as if I were outside myself, looking at myself through a kind of fog that was gradually clearing. And suddenly I knew that what I had been planning for that evening was so wrong, so out of key with my standards and my loyalties and the innermost me that it was out of the question.

"I remember standing there with the ax in my hand when this realization swept over me, dripping with perspiration, almost as if I had sweated the stupidity and selfishness out of me, along with the stale tobacco and alcohol. Then I plunged into the sea, and when I came out I felt clean and new and different. Later that day I called up the girl and canceled the date. Now what do you make of that?"

"You had a spiritual experience," I said.

"Spiritual, yes," he said. "But don't you see, I had to reach a point physically where the spiritual experience could happen. You know, I really believe that if every psychiatrist made every patient run around the block before stretching out on the couch, the incidence of emotional maladjustment in this country could be cut in half. And if we could just sell young people—and old ones too—on the excitement and pride and satisfactions involved in staying in good physical condition all their lives, we'd not only be a healthier nation, we'd be a more moral one."

"It does take willpower, though," I said, thinking of my own struggles through the years with the problem of second helpings.

He laughed. "Name me one worthwhile thing in this life that doesn't. Discipline is the price you pay for freedom. Come on; let's go get some breakfast!"

As I've indicated, that conversation took place several years ago. But I remember distinctly that one sentence: *Discipline is the price you pay for freedom.* Because it is profoundly true, and it is the heart of what I am trying to say in this book. Discipline is a liberator; it sets you free—free from the tyranny of laziness, of sloth, of flabbiness physical and mental, of harmful habits. Discipline restores your freedom of choice: you no longer *have* to have a cocktail at lunch, you no longer feel *compelled* to go out in the middle of the night in order to obtain a pack of cigarettes. When you are a disciplined person, authority is no longer forced upon you from without; it is something that you yourself control from within.

I remember very well that what my friend said on the beach that day made such an impression on me that I took a kind of inventory of my own performance in the area of physical fitness. And I wasn't terribly proud of what I found. I *was* too soft. I was overweight. I never had worked, really worked, at keeping my body in top physical condition. I found myself thinking of an old friend, William Danforth, the man who started what is now the Ralston Purina Company. He lived to a ripe old age in spite of being so frail as a child that he was told he probably couldn't live very long. But then a teacher, the kind who sees possibilities in boys and challenges them to realize them, said to young Danforth, "I dare you to be strong, I dare you to have a strong body, a strong mind and spirit." The boy responded to the dare with all the force he could muster. He literally took charge of his physique and made himself into a vigorous and healthy man, who lived a long and creative life. He wrote a little book called *I Dare You* which made men out of many boys across the years.

I was past the age where I could sensibly take up some

fast and competitive sport like handball, but there was one area where I could literally step up my pace without too much trouble, and that area was the neglected art of walking. Doctors will tell you that brisk walking exercises just about every muscle in your body. And I will add that it exercises quite a few muscles in your mind, too.

I began my experiment with serious walking in Switzerland, where I spend as much time each summer as my duties permit. And if there is a better place on this planet to walk, I don't know where it is. The summer air in Switzerland is clean and cool and bracing. The scenery is stupendous. You can walk in gentle valleys and look up at gigantic snow-covered peaks, or in a matter of minutes you can take a chair lift up several thousand feet, tramp along more rugged terrain, and look down at sapphire lakes lying far below. Sometimes you meet a herd of cows coming down from the high pastures, flowers wound in their horns, their great bells jangling. You walk for miles, feeling your soul expand along with your lungs.

For the first few days, you get so tired that you can barely wait for bedtime. Then, as you begin to toughen up, you walk farther and faster with less and less fatigue. At first you're afraid you can't make that climb, or cover that distance. But soon you know you can, and this confidence in what your body can do gives you a pride and satisfaction that spills over into your mental outlook. Difficulties seem to diminish, problems grow smaller, your reserves of energy come flooding back—and all because you're giving your work-hungry body the diet it needs, at last!

But the important thing is: it doesn't *have* to be walking. You can climb stairs instead of automatically taking the elevator. You can go bowling instead of to the movies. You can push a hand lawnmower instead of riding on a motorized one. You can take up bicycling again. A friend of mine likes to do push-ups, so he does an increasing number three times a day. Hardly takes him a minute, but the satisfaction he gets from knowing his arms, shoulders, stomach, muscles— and willpower—can do what he wants them to do, is, he claims, a very reassuring, confidence-building feeling. Another friend loves to garden—and works hard at it.

Better still, you can make yourself acquire the habit of daily scientific exercises. Many of my friends are completely sold on the system worked out by the Royal Canadian Air

Force which is available in most bookstores in booklet form. Carefully graded to suit age and physical condition, these exercises require just nine minutes each day—but to obtain real results and progress into higher categories you must do them *every* day.

Actually, where exercise is concerned, I think there are two levels of achievement. The first level, which is within anyone's reach, simply involves getting enough exercise to keep your muscles in good condition. The second level, which few of us ever fully attain, is the almost spiritual excitement that comes from demanding and getting maximum effort and performance from our physical selves.

One night at a dinner at the Explorers Club, I heard a famous mountain climber talk about this. "You seldom hear a real climber talk about the conquest of Everest," he said, "or of this mountain or that. Because it's not really the mountain that we're trying to conquer; it's ourselves. I've heard people say that we must have some kind of death-wish that makes us take such chances, but I think that's nonsense. And we're not out there to prove that we're not afraid of falling, or of freezing death, because of course we are. No, it's something else; it's a kind of desire to extract the last possible ounce of endurance and effort from ourselves. I imagine it's like trying to run a four-minute mile. If you've ever forced yourself to the absolute limit, and a bit beyond, there's a kind of exaltation about it that's indescribable. For that brief, intense, painful period of time, you're living fully, not just partially. And there's no other satisfaction like it in the world!"

This idea of the spiritual value of physical challenge is beginning to be recognized by educators. Out in Colorado, a summer school for boys and young men between the ages of sixteen and twenty-two has been receiving a lot of attention lately. Known as the Outward Bound School, it is based on a theory evolved in England, namely, that young people are bored by a sedentary, apathetic existence, that they welcome challenge even if it involves a rugged degree of physical hardship or more than a whiff of danger.

At the Outward Bound School, youngsters spend what may very well be the toughest month of their lives. Each day begins at 6 A.M. with a hard three-quarter-mile run followed by a plunge into an icy mountain pool. The boys have to become proficient at swinging along on a two hundred-foot aerial rope-course stretched high above the ground. They climb mountains and glaciers, carry forty-pound packs over one hundred-mile pack trips, go into the wilderness alone with only the barest equipment, and live off the country. They learn, in short, that they can do about three times as much—physically—as they ever dreamed they could do, and in the process they acquire enormous pride and confidence in themselves. The softness of civilization is burned away, and the true spirit of adventure is liberated. As one instructor says, "What we do with these boys is teach them to discover their maximum potential. It's tough while it lasts, but afterward not one of them would trade their experience for anything in the world."

The point is you *must* begin—you must take that first step, do that first push-up, swing that racket. Sometimes, being human, we put off that first step not just because we're lazy, but because we're afraid we won't succeed or will make fools of ourselves. Nonsense! No one expects you to be perfect, no one expects you to have the body of a Greek god. No one will laugh derisively at you. But they will do something— and that will be admire you tremendously. The other day, as I walked through Central Park, I saw a man—not much younger than I, and not too much thinner—trotting along the path in a gym suit. I stopped and stared—my mind filled with praise for that man who had the courage and wisdom and confidence to defy his fear of "what people might think" and undertake an experience he enjoyed and knew was good for him.

So, I urge you—right now—take that first step. Tell your wife to get her coat and go for a walk. Or, get out that exercise book, and do a few simple ones—but right now. Your kids may look askance—but soon admiration will filter through and, if you keep them up each day, they'll appreciate your willpower and, through you, gain some of their own.

In other words, the physical, mental, and emotional are so tied in together that I feel very safe in making you a promise: If you start, stick with, and enjoy some healthy exercise program, I promise you your whole attitude toward life, its problems and potential will change—for the far, far better.

Since discovering for myself, at least, this marvelous tie-in between the healthy mind and body, I've talked about the joys of exercise in more than one sermon and made a few converts, I hope. I have also put more emphasis on physical fitness in my counseling work, and people have told me that they found problems less menacing and their capacity for dealing with them much greater when they followed my suggestion that they be more conscientious about exercise, cut down or eliminate smoking and drinking, watch their diet.

These are the four areas that most people think of instinctively when you challenge them to be healthier than they are. And many people ignore the challenge because something in them resents being told what to do. They resist what seems to them like the voice of authority. And yet, they are already the victims of an authority far more despotic than the advice of a well-meaning counselor. The smoker is the servant of his little white cylinder; the drinker is the captive of the depressant known as alcohol; the glutton is the slave of his own appetite; the flabby person is imprisoned in his own fat. Again, only the truly disciplined person is truly free.

I try to make this point very strongly in my counseling because, as I have said before, purely negative arguments seem to have little effect on people. You have to appeal to the pride, to the latent *nobility*, that lurks in every human being. You don't say, "You should really give up this habit because it may hurt you." You say: "Breaking this habit will be difficult and demanding and tough. Some people aren't strong enough to do it. But I think you are. What do you think?" Then, if they give you back even a feeble affirmative, you have to pounce on it, bang your fist on the desk if necessary, drive that idea deep into their subconscious by saying, "Of course you are! You are God's child, and made in His image, and whenever you reach for a decision that is good, enormous power is available to you. With His help you can do it and you will do it!"

Very often people who want to make a move in the right direction are unconsciously waiting for a push to get them started. I used to smoke myself, when I was a youngster in college, and I began to wonder if the habit might not be getting a permanent hold on me. I voiced these fears to my younger brother Bob, who is now a physician. "This craving for nicotine can be a powerful thing," I said gloomily. But Bob is a blunt and forthright individual. "Craving, my foot!" he said. "It's all a state of mind. If you want to give it up, take charge of yourself and give it up!" I did.

Obviously, it's much easier never to start smoking than it is to stop. Therefore I think parents have a definite obligation to dissuade their children from starting. One of the best ways is by example. If a boy's father doesn't smoke, and he admires his father, there is a good chance that he won't smoke either. But it's also possible to appeal to a youngster's good sense, or even his sense of humor. I remember saying to my son John that if a desire for something harmful didn't exist in his life, why go to a lot of trouble and expense to acquire it? First attempts at smoking, I pointed out, were almost invariably unpleasant. "To develop a taste for smoking just so that you can satisfy it," I told him, "seems a little like dousing yourself with itching powder just so that you can scratch!" He laughed and said that this seemed pretty silly to him, too. And that was the end of it: John doesn't smoke, either.

Drinking, of course, is a far more complex and formidable problem than smoking. A heavy smoker harms only himself. A heavy drinker can not only wreck his own life but ruin the lives of people around him. "Drink has taken five million men and women in the United States, taken them as masters take slaves, and new acquisitions are going on at the rate of 200,000 a year," says the *Journal of the American Medical Association*. If figures are correct, and I feel sure they are, and if you assume that each alcoholic twists and distorts at least three other lives, which I'm sure is a conservative number, then at least *twenty million* Americans are victims directly or indirectly of this dreadful affliction.

Actually alcohol is neither good nor bad, any more than a pistol or an automobile is. It's the way it's used that counts. Many people are able to use it with no visible harm to themselves or others. But the record shows that sooner or later one out of fifteen "social" drinkers will become an alcoholic. And the consequences are devastating to the person and to society.

I believe the chief reason people drink—or smoke, for that matter—is that these activities have a narcotic effect that reduces tension. Tension, or anxiety, is an unpleasant thing to experience; it is a kind of psychic pain. All of us have to live with some of it. When it becomes severe, it takes a strong and integrated personality to endure it.

It would seem to me, therefore, that the best approach to the problem would be to concentrate on producing strong, well-balanced, tension-resistant people, rather than trying (unsuccessfully, for the most part) to keep alcohol out of reach. I believe religion has a great role to play here, because the truly religious person who lives and feels he is loved by God is much less likely to be haunted by anxiety than a person who does not. And I also believe that, in proportion as a person learns to discipline and control himself, his tensions will diminish. Why not? To a great extent, the disciplined person controls his life and his environment. He doesn't have to be afraid of it.

One woman I know, who gave up both drinking and smoking, told me how she did it. "Every time I took a drink or lit a cigarette," she said, "I asked myself this question: 'Are you gaining control, or losing it?' It was pretty obvious to me that after one drink I had less power of choice when it came to deciding about another drink. I was losing control, not gaining it. As for cigarettes, when I felt a strong urge to light one, and gave in to that urge, I was surrendering my freedom of choice again. I finally decided that life is complicated enough without these petty tyrants interfering with your freedom and pushing you around. So I made up my mind to get rid of them altogether, and I did!"

She made up her mind; that was the secret. Nobody forced her, nobody directed her to do it; the direction came from within. *She made up her mind;* there's something triumphantly final about that phrase. It excludes all doubt; it brushes hesitancy aside. That woman didn't sit around wondering if giving up two bad habits might be a good idea. She didn't ask herself if she could do it. She didn't consult her friends. She just made a decision and nailed it up in her mind and proceeded from then on to act differently.

Believe me, there's nothing like the satisfaction that comes from this sort of inner-directedness. I know, because a few years ago I had to wage a little private war of my own, and my adversary was my own fondness for food. As a youngster I was thin as a rake, and even as a young minister I can remember—incredibly—drinking double malted milks in an effort to look more substantial. Furthermore, growing up on some of the richest farmland in America, populated by some of the best cooks, I had plenty of opportunity to become intimately acquainted with heaping platters of crisp fried chicken, snowy mounds of mashed potatoes dripping with butter, glossy pork roasts with crackling fat, biscuits smothered in rich gravy, and so on.

This happy intimacy did me no harm until I reached my fortieth birthday. But then suddenly it began to do me no good at all. Almost before I knew it, I was struggling, like millions of Americans, in the quicksands of overweight.

They say that the only exercise that really affects this problem is the exercise involved in firmly pushing yourself away from the dinner table. This is probably true, but before you can do that effectively you have to exercise something else, and that's your willpower. Or rather, your won't-power. Again, nobody can make you do this. Your doctor may tell you ominously, as mine told me, that for every extra pound of excess weight your heart has to pump blood through additional *miles* of microscopic blood vessels. None of these things will produce the desired change in you unless on some deep level you want that change so badly that you demand it of yourself. When you reach the necessary intensity of demand, you find that your demon appetite submits and submits quite meekly.

How do you reach that intensity of self-demand? In a variety of ways. In my own struggle to reduce, I made use of several different techniques. And needed them all, I might add!

The first step is to try to analyze your problem—honestly! Ask yourself *why* you're overeating, overdrinking, etc. Is it simply because you're fond of good food and have grown accustomed to taking the line of least resistance? Is it possible that you are resentful of something or somebody and are eating because it seems to reduce your anger? Is it conceivable that you are starved for affection and are finding a substitute in food? Are you running away from the normal problems of life, reaching for a sweet—as one doctor put it —instead of a solution?

Sometimes a compulsive overeater may need help in making such an analysis, help from his pastor, his doctor, even a psychiatrist. But if he can pinpoint the cause of his problem and start working to eliminate it, he will have won half the battle right there. For instance, many of our most seriously bad eating habits are incubated when we are young. Think back, and perhaps like me, you'll recall that you *had* to "clean your plate," that you were bad if you didn't, good if you did. And weren't you rewarded with food, deprived for punishment? In other words, food took on more than just a caloric value; it became a symbol of love and acceptance, and, therefore, today, you may overeat to gain love—rather than energy. I know a man who, to this day, can't resist raiding a refrigerator—anyone's, really—because he was never allowed to, when young, and so being able to eat left-overs from the refrigerator in some way makes this fellow feel secure. Sounds strange, even amazing, but it's not—and it *is* a more general problem than you think. Ponder it next time you are about to eat *more* than you need!

One of the most successful control devices is to see yourself as you want to be. Imagination is stronger even than willpower, because it can sink into the unconscious mind and bring about changes that willpower unaided cannot always achieve.

For years I have been preaching—and both the Bible and modern psychiatry bear me out—that a basic fact of human nature is our tendency to become like that which we habitually imagine ourselves to be. "As [a man] thinketh in his heart," says the Bible, "so is he." In other words, any deeply held mental picture tends to realize itself in fact. If you think of yourself as a defeated person, you tend to activate negative forces that work toward producing defeat. If you conceive of yourself as a victorious person, you stimulate creative forces that push you on to victory.

Decide, then, on how you would like to look. Don't dwell on the way you are; concentrate on the way you would like to be. Picture yourself as slender, active, alert. "See" yourself at a certain weight, possessing a certain waist measurement. Peg that picture up in your mind and concentrate on it. Presently your unconscious mind will accept this image. And whatever lies deeply imbedded in the unconscious you will have, because it has you!

After a speech I had made in a West Coast city, a woman waddled up to me. I use this rather inelegant word because it accurately describes the impression this very obese lady made on me. I was startled when she asked, "How old do you think I am?"

"Well now, madam," I replied. "I may not appear very bright, but I am not so stupid as to go around guessing women's ages and announcing my conclusions."

"No," she persisted. "I mean it. I really want you to tell me how old you think I am."

Finally, convinced of her seriousness and concluding she had some real purpose in this strange request, I considered the matter and said, "Well, let's say fifty years old."

With a triumphant look she said, "Actually, I'm thirty-six and the thing that gives me that fifty-year-old look is this awful weight. What I want to know is how I can get it down to where it should be and look more nearly my age."

It came out in discussion that her power of will was about as flabby as her arm, which hung down in a huge roll of fat. "It seems the more I eat, the more I want and can eat," she explained. "My doctor says what happens to overweight people is that their stomachs stretch to accommodate their appetites."

I asked her if she could paint a mental picture of what she would like to be, explaining that a mental picture explicitly described and strongly held tends to motivate action that will finally develop into fact.

She at once assured me that she would like to weigh 125 pounds and have a waist measurement of 24 and bust measurement of 34. Furthermore she would like to attain this by New Year's Day, which was about eight months away.

I liked the decisiveness of her self-picture and told her she had taken the first step. She was on her way to becoming what she imagined. She must hold that self-image strongly in consciousness and believe absolutely in its realizability.

Of course that was not all. Equally strong follow-through thoughts had to be set in motion. She was especially fond of "gooey desserts," she told me, and had been known to eat a pound box of chocolates at one sitting. So I told her we would tackle first the gooey desserts. Looking at one of these calorie-reeking desserts, she was to estimate how long it would take her to eat it—she thought probably three minutes. Then, she was to think how proud and happy she would feel at the end of those crucial minutes if she had passed up the dessert and had not eaten it. She would experience for the first time the thrill of self-mastery.

Subsequently, every dessert, every chocolate, every piece of cake that she had not eaten would give her a delightful taste of satisfaction. At night when she was ready to say her prayers she was to run over the day mentally, add up all the fattening things she had not eaten, and then eagerly look forward to seeing how she could top this the next day. Then she was to thank God for the wonderful fun she was having and go to sleep in the joy of a job well done.

She wrote to me from time to time reporting progress and telegraphed me on New Year's Day that she had hit 127 pounds and added "I'll get those other two, believe me." Over a year later I was speaking in a Los Angeles hotel ballroom at a convention. After the end of the meeting, suddenly an attractive young woman stood before me and with a big smile she asked, "Tell me, how old do I look to you?" I stared. Sure enough, it was she but I wouldn't have known her at all. There she stood, a dedicated self-image come true.

In the last analysis, both the spirit and the body have to be toughened by discipline and self-denial if the full potential of a human being is to be realized. If the body is too weak, the spirit cannot drive it beyond a certain point. And if the will is lacking, the strongest muscles in the world will not respond to challenge.

But when the will is strong and the body is strong there is almost nothing that a person cannot do. America was built by strong-willed, strong-muscled men; our history is full of their exploits. Let me end this chapter by recalling one of them. I happened to be reading about him just the other night.

This man's name was John Phillips, but everyone called him Portugee Phil. He was a civilian scout with the United States Army in the turbulent days just after the Civil War when the Indians of the Western plains realized that they had no choice but to fight or be overrun by the tide of white settlers sweeping west.

In December 1866, the Sioux were on the warpath under their great chief, Red Cloud. With their allies, the Cheyennes, they were trying to stop the whites from building a string of forts along the Powder River from Fort Laramie to the gold fields of Montana. In what is now northern Wyoming, they had the little garrison at Fort Kearny under virtual siege.

A fiery young officer, Captain William Fetterman, said to his commander, "Give me eighty men and I'll ride through the whole Sioux nation!" He got his eighty men, was decoyed into an ambush, and massacred with his entire command. Not a man escaped. One officer was found with 120 arrows in his body.

This left the garrison at Fort Kearny in a desperate plight. That night a raging blizzard sent the temperature down to thirty below zero. The commander knew that the storm would prevent an Indian attack for the moment, but he also knew he had to have reinforcements. He called for volunteers to ride through the blizzard and through the ring of blood-crazed Indians for help. And Portugee Phil Phillips volunteered.

Now, this man was not in the Army. He was not under orders. He valued his life as much as any man. But something in his mind or his heart made him stand up and say that he thought he could do it.

He took the garrison commander's horse, a magnificent Kentucky hunter, and plunged into the swirling snow. The wind cut his face; the sleet froze in his nostrils. The horse's hoofbeats rang on frozen rivers or were muffled by drifts four feet deep. He did not dare stop for rest or food. All day and all night he struggled on until he came at dawn to another outpost, Fort Reno.

But Reno had no telegraph, and no troops it could spare. So, with a fresh horse, Phillips plunged on. Not far from Reno a band of Indians chased him, but he outrode them. On he went, all day and all night, until he reached Horseshoe Station.

Here there was a telegraph, and a message was sent to Laramie. But Phillips was afraid that the wires might be down (as indeed they were) and that the message might not get through. So again he hurled himself into the storm, on and on, hour after agonizing hour. That night, a dying horse stumbled up to the gates of Laramie. The rider slid off, a grotesque, snow-encrusted figure. Men ran to help him, but he waved them off. Not until he had handed his dispatches to the commanding officer did his iron will falter. Then he fell unconscious to the floor. Within hours, troops were on their way to Fort Kearny.

Three days and three nights. Two hundred and thirty-six miles under conditions that would have killed most men. Two chances to give up with honor and safety—both rejected.

When you read or hear of something like this, doesn't a kind of thrill go shivering down your spine? It does down mine. Doesn't it make you feel a little ashamed of your preoccupation with security and comfort and safety and convenience? It does me. Can't we modern Americans, by disciplining our minds and bodies, reach back and recapture a part of this magnificent heritage of ours?

I think we must. I hope we can.

Outer Pressures and Inner Braces

I've always remembered a story someone told me years ago about one of our more colorful congressional leaders, the late Martin Barnaby Madden of Illinois. It seems that near the end of his long and distinguished career, Representative Madden observed that a certain young congressman was often voting as pressure groups dictated. He also noticed that this young man would never express open dissent with anyone, but always agreed affably with whatever was being said.

Congressman Madden spoke of this to the younger man, who admitted that he had this fault. "But," he said, "you know how it is, Mr. Madden. The external pressures on us legislators are tremendous."

"Young man," said Madden, "I know all about the outer pressures. But where are your inner braces?"

It's a story I have repeated many times to people facing moral choices of one kind or another. Very often, in the face of temptation, you can't control the outer pressures. But you can do a lot about your inner braces. You can study yourself and get to know your areas of weakness. You can try to strengthen these weak places by self-discipline and self-denial and prayer. You can build up your moral resistance with spiritual exercises just the way you can build up your body with physical exercises. Then when the moral pressures of life come, gradually or suddenly, you'll not only be able to endure them, but actually grow stronger by enduring them.

In talking with his colleague, Congressman Madden was dealing with a specific kind of immorality: immorality in government. And this is the area of human affairs that I want to discuss in the next chapter. Perhaps you'll find such a discussion a bit startling, or think it out of place in a book of this kind. But I really don't see how any book attempting to deal with man as an inner-directed being can avoid it, because the form of government under which he lives often determines just how inner-directed a man can be. It can liberate and encourage that capacity, or it can stifle it.

And so, in discussing morality in government, I shall not be concerned with the occasional corrupt official who is dishonest on the personal level. I don't intend to discuss the relative merits of political personalities or parties, either. What I hope to do is discuss fundamental philosophies of government that seem to me moral or immoral insofar as they affect for good or ill this capacity for self-direction among tens of millions of people.

I think such a discussion belongs in this book. As Rousseau said two centuries ago: "Those who would treat politics and morality apart will never understand the one or the other."

He was right.

CHAPTER IX

Politics and Morality

The story goes that when the Founding Fathers of this nation emerged from the session where they had put the final touches on the Constitution, some of the waiting crowd buttonholed Benjamin Franklin. "What have you given us?" they asked anxiously. "A republic," said old Ben, "if you can keep it!"

I think it's crystal clear what the wise old statesman meant. He meant that a republic is such a delicately balanced form of government, surrounded by so many dangers and pitfalls, that whether or not it survives depends entirely on the character of its citizens. Not, ultimately, on how much prosperity they have. Not on how much security they have. But on their toughness, vigilance, intelligence, energy, selflessness, honesty, and patriotism . . . in other words, their *character*.

Franklin had lived through the Revolution. He had seen his country born. And he foresaw a great future for it. But he was also aware of the danger that has always been inherent in a free society, the danger that independence will lead to prosperity, and prosperity to laxness and softness and indifference, and these in turn to loss of freedom. That was why his answer was, "A republic, if you can keep it."

Well, almost two centuries have passed, and we still have our republic. But we have kept it, I think, because we have never ceased asking ourselves searching questions. Is our nation growing stronger or is it growing weaker? Are the checks and balances built into the Constitution still working? Are our citizens as free now as they were fifty or a hundred years ago? Are the forces that made this country great as strong as ever? Is our star still rising or has it begun to wane? From the beginning Americans have asked these questions and sometimes disagreed passionately over the answers. But disagreement is not the danger. The danger is that men will stop asking the questions and trying to answer them, that they will say to their leaders, "Oh, you decide; I'm too busy." Or, "It's too complicated." Or simply, "Who cares?"

It seems to me that the fundamental question in politics today is this: How much government is good government? Assuming a reasonable amount of honesty, good will, and good sense on the part of our elected or appointed officials, do we want the role of government in our lives to grow greater or less?

The fact that I raise this question does not, I hope, make me a misanthropic reactionary, a chronic viewer-with-alarm, or a one-man committee fanatically dedicated to turning back clocks. I am aware that big government is with us, and that it is here to stay. I realize that it requires massive federal funds to proceed, say, with the exploration of outer space. I can see much good in some big government projects—the Peace Corps, for example, which I think has done and is doing a great deal to help people—and incidentally to combat Communism all over the world. Sometimes we need the weight of government to carry out needed reforms. I was proud of our country when the Congress passed the law guaranteeing civil rights to all our citizens. This was a long overdue and profoundly moral act. It indicates that in great issues big government can take an affirmative position in matters of basic morality and humanity.

There must be progress and there must be improvement in our society, and I am well aware that it takes a big government to run a big country and bring about big changes. But I also think that government can become *too* paternalistic. And I am deeply concerned lest this ultimately bring about a fundamental change in the character of the American people.

Because—make no mistake about it—the greatness of America is based on the character of its individual citizens. Three hundred years ago this country was a wilderness. Two hundred years ago it was a handful of colonial villages. One hundred years ago it was torn by a Civil War so murderous and exhausting that it would have destroyed a lesser nation. Today, with only 5 or 6 percent of the people in the world, it produces over half the total wealth of the planet and has shared that wealth with friends, former enemies, and dubious neutrals in the most extraordinary display of generosity in the history of mankind. I mention this generosity because, while amassing wealth and producing things may not be among the noblest measures of a nation, willingness to share those products of ingenuity and effort certainly is.

What made all this happen? Natural resources? It is true that we have them, but so does Siberia, so does the Congo. Climate? There is nothing unique about ours. Geography? Our nation gains no more advantage from its position between two oceans than our neighbors do. Freedom from devastation of war? Brazil has been equally free. In other words, if any *material* advantages exist, they are too slight to come anywhere near accounting for the disparity in performance. So the answer must lie in our spiritual or our political heritage . . . possibly both.

Let's consider our spiritual heritage first. Despite the high attendance that our churches claim today, I believe that in the eighteenth and nineteenth centuries America was a more deeply religious nation than it is now. People read the Bible with deep attention and tried to base their lives on its teaching. How many people actually do this today? All these things gave a moral tincture to life, a framework of right and wrong that may have been rigid but also served to release people's energies. History tells us that when people deny themselves licentiousness and immorality in the name of religion or the name of anything else, they have greater energy, enterprise, and daring than those who give in to self-indulgence. Our ancestors were not dissipated people, they were focused people—and religion was the great lens that kept them focused.

But religion could not have been the only factor; other countries have been—and are—just as religious as ours. Some other great intangible must have been at work, pulsing through men's minds, singing through their hearts, releasing the torrents of energy that in a few short decades tamed the wilderness and harnessed the rivers and built the cities and factories and churches and schools and universities that in turn poured their own energies into the great current.

What was it? What was the key that unlocked this amazing dynamism? I think it can be defined in two words: personal freedom. Such freedom had existed before, here and there, like a flickering flame in the darkness of oppression and tyranny. But in most places, in most times, the common man had only such freedom as his governors saw fit to grant him. Nowhere had the idea really taken root that government was entitled only to such power as the citizen saw fit to grant it. Certainly such an idea had never been handed to men who stood poised on the edge of a mighty continent waiting to be conquered and controlled and turned into productivity and power.

There were not very many of them, back in 1783, perhaps four million or so. Most of them very poor, few were wealthy or powerful. But for more than a century they and their ancestors had been seeking freedom of one kind or another—freedom from political oppression, freedom from religious persecution, freedom from class distinctions, from exploitation by old and outmoded forms of government. And when by the grace of God (as they believed, and so do I) they won their struggle against the most powerful nation in the world and found themselves, incredibly, an independent and sovereign nation, it was almost as if a mighty Voice said to them, "Now you have your freedom. Put it to work." And they did, with a zeal and fire and enthusiasm that became the wonder and envy of the world.

It was never easy. I believe it is almost impossible for us pampered children of the twentieth century to conceive of what it was like—say—to clear and plough an acre of virgin forest, or plod with a wagon train across the mountains and the deserts. But hardship, challenge, and struggle—painful in themselves—can also unlock tremendous reservoirs in the human spirit, if that spirit is independent and unsubdued. That was the spirit they had, the spirit that built America.

Why were they able to maintain it, decade after decade? Because the pioneer fringe, the cutting edge, remained lean and hard and hungry. Because they were able to work for themselves and their families without interference or restriction. Because they were proud of the independence they had won (consider how they celebrated the Fourth of July!), and jealous of it, and determined that it should not be lost or whittled away again.

And with this independence went, I think, a kind of rough idealism. A man was judged not so much by what he had as what he was. Wealth was a useful thing to have, and fine if you could get it, but integrity was more important. Duty, honor, loyalty—these were not just high-sounding words, but qualities that some men sought and found, and all men responded to with admiration and respect.

I'm not trying to say that this early American way of life had no faults; it did. There was poverty. There was exploitation of labor by capital. There were sweatshops and child labor, and redlight districts and drunkenness, and other social evils. But these were challenged and fought, even then, by the churches and the benevolent societies and enlightened individuals who understood that where there is independence there must also be responsibility. "Although the world is full of suffering," Helen Keller has said, "it is full of the overcoming of it." And that process, without benefit of governmental intervention, was going on then.

Was that process too slow? Perhaps. The struggle against evil always seems to take too much time. My point is that for five generations after achieving independence Americans clung to the goals they had fought for. The main targets of our Revolution were arbitrary government and unrepresentative taxation. With these eliminated, we kept our government sharply limited and our taxes low. We paid off our national debts even after the Civil War and the First World War. But in the last generation all this changed.

Back in 1910, when I was a happy sixth-grader in Ohio, the population of this country was about ninety million, the cost of running the federal government was about one billion, and the national debt was one billion. Today our population has doubled, but the cost of running the government is around one hundred billion dollars a year, and the national debt is over three hundred billion. In other words, forgetting inflation for the moment, it is costing us one hundred times as much to govern twice as many people as it did half a century ago. And we owe ourselves three hundred times as much now as we did then.

What got us into such a fix? For one thing, our humanitarian instincts did. It troubled our conscience, as it should have, to see people ill-clothed and ill-housed and ill-fed. If correcting these evils meant that we had to go into debt, we would do it.

But then debt became a habit, and now it is accepted as a way of life. I know that if you voice a layman's plea for fiscal sanity in the more sophisticated liberal circles you are regarded as a quaint and not-too-bright fossil. The country's economy is so strong, they will tell you, that it can easily carry a little old debt of three hundred billion dollars, which after all, if you could see it in cash, would only make a stack of one-thousand-dollar bills thirty-seven miles high.

Well, I may be naïve, and I'll admit that I seldom see in the collection plate a stack of bills over three inches high, but it seems to me that somebody is going to have to foot that bill sooner or later, unless we plan to repudiate it, which would be an act of colossal immorality in itself.

People are strangely apathetic and fatalistic about this. It's almost as if we had persuaded ourselves that somebody else owes the money, not ourselves. But we *are* the government, and the debt as it stands today amounts to an average of over six thousand dollars for every family in the United States. And don't think each of us isn't paying the interest in the form of taxes because we are, at the rate of eleven billion dollars per year, which is more than three times as much as the government spent for all purposes between 1925 and 1930.

Something is wrong here, you can't persuade me that it isn't. If our generation, which is spending this borrowed money, simply hands on the debt to future generations who have not incurred it, this doesn't seem a very moral procedure to me. And if—as is already happening—we pay back the trusting holders of government bonds in currency that has depreciated 43 percent in the last twenty years, that doesn't strike me as very moral either.

In the long run this fairly obvious immorality may not be as damaging to the soul of America as the relentless pressure that big money in Washington exerts both on those who disburse it and those who receive it. If the government is costing us over one hundred billion dollars per year, this means that every single week close to two billions are being spent somewhere, a state of affairs that tends to create an ever-increasing horde of official donors on the one hand and a too-dependent class of citizens on the other. With rivers of gold flowing from Washington, the temptation to clamor for a share of it becomes irresistible, and too often the clamor is justified, not on the grounds that the money is urgently needed, but that it's there, it's being spent, and those who don't get theirs are just plain stupid. The idea that a local community can and should pay for its own improvements and control its own affairs becomes first narcotized and eventually forgotten.

You don't have to be a political expert, or even very interested in politics, to see that under these circumstances the pressures on individual congressmen become enormous. On the one hand his constituents back home are urging him to grab what he can from the public trough and threatening to withhold their votes from him unless he does. Meantime in

Washington any administration which controls the spending has a ready-made device for bribing him into voting the way they want him to vote.

This "subsidy seduction" or "ballot bribery," as it has been called, has become so common that it barely raises an eyebrow any longer. Some congressmen, in fact, become highly indignant if anyone questions the morality of their attempts to divert large sums of money belonging to all the people to benefit a small minority of the people, namely, their constituents back home.

This same kind of sectional favoritism becomes glaringly apparent whenever an attempt is made to eliminate an obsolete military establishment or reduce topheavy government stockpiles by selling surplus commodities. Trying to get a congressman to approve the elimination of a military establishment in his district on the grounds that it would promote the national welfare is like trying to take meat away from a saber-toothed tiger. Trying to reduce a stockpile brings anguished screams and vehement lobbying from the industry producing that particular commodity.

These are some of the disadvantages of too much centralization of financial power. Of course, despite these things, we have national prosperity. More people have more money, more cars, more television sets, more washing machines. And yet I seem to sense, beneath all this proud prosperity, a kind of emptiness, a kind of purposelessness, a kind of hunger in people as if something deep and basic were not being satisfied. We have plenty of bread, and plenty of circuses on credit. But man doesn't live by bread alone, and circuses satisfy only the senses, not the soul. Man needs involvement with life. He needs closeness with other men. He needs a great cause to live for and if necessary to die for. You don't get that from television sets and washing machines.

Why is it that in Sweden, where the state sees to it that everyone has material security from the cradle to the grave, the alcoholism and suicide rates are among the highest in the world? Why is it that in Ireland, one of the poorer Western nations, these rates are among the lowest? Could it be that in Ireland, where life is still harsh and tough for many people, men are still individuals, not simply faceless consumers of security? I wonder.

It is that sort of wondering that most of us must do, together or separately, if we are to be effective citizens of a republic. It's not enough just to accept political party labels and affiliations. You have to go deeper, down to the fundamental philosophies of government, and take your stand on whatever moral bedrock you can find there.

This is a terribly difficult assignment, because there are no simple answers. How can there be in a world where global communications have become instantaneous, where the cushions of time and space no longer exist, where the onrush of technology has lifted living standards in some areas of our planet to unprecedented heights while leaving others as backward and benighted as ever? Terrifying questions loom above us, ranging from the present menace of Communism to the future menace of the population explosion, from the threats to individual liberty today to the threat of extinction under the mushroom cloud of radiation tomorrow. The questions are so huge and so menacing that the mind reels and the spirit quails before them.

But the mind cannot afford to reel, and the spirit must somehow summon up the courage to grapple with them. In each generation there must be men and women brave enough and independent enough and self-disciplined enough to face these questions and attempt to solve them.

They must also be people with faith in other people, because the fundamental question that must be answered is this: can man control himself or must he be controlled? If the average man is merely a self-centered animal concerned only with his own welfare and security, devoid of patriotism, scornful of honor, then perhaps the answer must be "Yes, he must be controlled." But I don't believe this. I believe that the average man—and I am one—needs to be educated and persuaded toward his responsibilities, and sometimes reminded of them. But I certainly do not think he is a grasping, selfish, stupid clod. I think there is in him a divine spark that makes him want to be generous and decent and independent and self-reliant and free. I believe that it is deeply immoral to attempt to blunt these instincts in him, or to assume that he does not have them. As Abraham Lincoln once said, "You cannot build character and courage by taking away man's initiative and independence. You cannot help men permanently by doing for them what they could and should do for themselves."

Self-responsibility—the thing I have been talking about in this book from the start—that is the key. Each of us must acquire it and display it if our perilous experiment with a republican form of government is to go forward. We can never delegate this responsibility to big government, or big business, or big labor, or any other gigantic father-image, however benevolent, however powerful, however competent they may seem. We must not only be willing to make our own decisions and govern our own affairs, we must insist on the right to do so, and fight for that right with ideas, with education, with persuasion, with exhortation, with the ballot, with any legitimate weapon we can lay our hands on.

Only thus can we reach full self-realization as responsible human beings. And only thus will our country, as we know and love it, continue to endure.

Dialogue in the Dark

Not long ago, late at night in a western city, I boarded an airliner to return to New York. The cabin lights were dim. My seat companion was a shadowy figure who lifted his briefcase from the seat I was to occupy, spoke pleasantly in a cultured voice, then sat quietly as we took off into the starlit night.

It was well past midnight, but for some reason I was not sleepy. So as the great plane rushed eastward I snapped on my overhead light, put my own briefcase on my knees, took out a pencil, and began to work on a draft of the chapter you have just read.

Evidently my companion wasn't sleepy either, because when I paused after an hour or so he asked me what I was doing. I told him about the book, and the series of challenges I hoped it contained.

"It sounds interesting," he said. "I'm sure that each of us is facing a moral challenge of one kind or another. But tell me, which do you consider the most widespread moral issue of our time, the one that is touching the lives of the greatest number of people?"

That made me stop and think a bit. But I did not have to search far for an answer. "I believe the most widespread moral problem today," I said, "is the problem of prejudice—the racial prejudice that has provoked so much anger and bitterness, and even bloodshed and death."

"Have you a chapter on race prejudice?" he asked.

"Actually," I replied, "every chapter, every word is about the subject. I'm trying to help people see themselves, face themselves, and fulfill themselves. If they do this, prejudice will vanish. Until they do, people will try to escape themselves by finding fault with others. When people set themselves up in judgment over other people, the assumption that they themselves are guiltless is usually false. That's what

Jesus meant when He warned us to get rid of the beam in our own eye before complaining too much about the mote in our neighbor's."

"But you have to take a stand against evil," he said.

"Yes, you do," I agreed. "You have to believe in the dignity of man, and set yourself against anything that tends to diminish that dignity. You have to believe that human personality is sacred, and fight against anything that tends to degrade it."

"People keep looking for simple answers," he said. "I'm afraid there aren't any."

"Christianity has an answer," I said. "It commands us to love our neighbor. It says that we are all children of God, and that since we have a common Father, we are all brothers. It's just as simple—and as deep and difficult—as that."

"It's difficult, all right," he said. "Prejudice takes root in people early, and it's terribly hard to dig it out. Take me, for instance: I like to think that I'm not prejudiced in any way. But when I put myself under the microscope of complete self-honesty, I know there are some dark areas where I think less of other men because they're unlike me. Prejudice can be such a subtle thing! I believe it would be quite possible to march in a civil rights demonstration and then go home feeling prejudiced against people who didn't march!"

"Exactly," I said. "You've got to go beyond pious attitudes. You've got to realize constantly that the shadow of the evil you are opposing exists within yourself. You can't be content with judging the other fellow—that's too easy. You've got to remember that the only person you can really change is you."

My newfound friend was silent for a moment. "That's true," he said finally. "Any decent person can feel anger and revulsion when some fellow citizen is brutalized, or treated unfairly in the courts, or denied the right to vote. But to realize that within yourself there is a little coiled snake of contempt for your neighbor because he's a Negro, or a Protestant, or a Catholic, or a Jew—or maybe because he's *not* any of these things—that's the real challenge. And to meet it takes real self-honesty, real self-discipline, real self-control."

I smiled to myself at his choice of words. They had been my companions for many long weeks as I worked on this book.

"What can we do?" he went on. "I mean, how can we go

beyond this smug stage of indignation over the failings of others? It's so easy to get bogged down there."

This time it was my turn to be silent for a few moments. The great plane still rushed through the night, filled with a sense of power and purpose. Far ahead of us, now, on the horizon, was a brilliant streak of crimson. Dawn was speeding toward us at a thousand miles per hour, and the plane seemed to be racing to meet it.

"I think," I said slowly, "that at any point in our lives each of us is standing on a kind of moral ladder. There are rungs above us, and rungs below. We can climb up, or we can step down. Or we can simply stand still, which is the easiest thing to do, because it requires no effort and involves no risk. Merely feeling indignant about the shortcomings of others is really a kind of moral standing-still. It's too passive; too easy. What we really have to do is make up our minds to move up a rung in the ladder, and begin to act differently in our own lives. Does the color of some person's skin tend to block you from normal relationship with him? Go out of your way to perform some little act of helpfulness or kindness. Do you resent your fellow worker because he got a promotion that you wanted for yourself? Tell him that you have been jealous, but that you are putting that behind you and that you wish him well. Are you giving one of your children more love than another? Make yourself quietly balance the books. In other words, take a step upward, however small."

"I suppose," my friend said, "the size of the step will vary with the individual."

"Naturally," I said. "You can't judge these things quantitatively. A southern housewife, let's say makes up her mind to call her Negro maid by the title of Miss or Mrs., instead of by her first name only. To a housewife in Nevada, this might seem absurdly small—almost nothing. But to a Mississippi housewife it might be the most significant step upward that she has ever taken. And actually it would be significant on scale because it would represent an acknowledgment of what I was talking about earlier—the infinite value of each human being, the common brotherhood of all of us, the dignity of man."

Ahead of us now the whole sky flamed azure and gold. In the growing light, I could see my companion's face clearly, a thoughtful face with little lines of humor and kindness, and a touch of honest worry too. He could have been a banker or a lawyer or an engineer or a teacher or a preacher or a doctor. He could have been any of these things and still shared a thousand thoughts and problems and reactions with me simply because we were both citizens of this troubled century.

He said, "Do you think we'll ever lick this prejudice business? Do you believe the different races and creeds will ever live together happily and harmoniously, the way God intended?"

I looked down through the luminous air at the great tapestry of America unrolling beneath us. Even as I looked, light was spilling over the rim of the world, driving the shadows away. I felt a sudden surge of confidence, a great uplifting of my heart and spirit—I don't know why, but I felt it.

"Yes," I said to my Negro seat companion, "I believe it. That's the dream and the promise. Some day they will come true."

MEMO TO THE READER NO. 9

The Five Wizard Words

A few years back I wrote a book about positive thinking that surprised me by being quite a success. It seemed to help a lot of people, and I received many letters of praise which —naturally—pleased me very much.

I also got some pretty sharp criticism from people who prided themselves on their intellectualism and sophistication. Positive thinking, these critics said loftily, was too down-to-earth, too simplified, too much of a cliché to do anyone any good. It was lifting yourself by your mental bootstraps. It was wishful thinking. It was this, it was that.

Well, when you're the target of criticism, it's a good idea to listen to what the critics say and try to evaluate it honestly. But it's also interesting, at the same time, to evaluate the critics, try to figure out what makes them so critical or so hostile.

I must confess, I haven't given too much time or thought to this, but it does seem to me that there is a curious tendency on the part of people who consider themselves superior in education or intellect to look down their noses at anything that is popular, anything that is simple (and most truth is simple), anything that touches the heart as well as the head.

Take this scorn of a cliché, for example. What, actually, is wrong with a good cliché? The fact that it is familiar simply means that it expresses an idea so well that it has become *the* handle that people prefer to use. Is this so bad? I don't think so.

As for positive thinking, I still believe in it completely. Countless people have told me that it has changed their lives for the better. Countless people have used and are using it to overcome fears and inadequacies and weaknesses. "A man," said Emerson, "is what he thinks about all day long." This is one way of expressing a deep spiritual law, the law that says: "Good thoughts drive out bad."

They do, you know. Positive thoughts drive out negative thoughts. Faith thoughts drive out doubt thoughts. Courage thoughts banish fear thoughts. If a strong thought meets a weak thought inside your head, it is going to chase it out. But you have to give the strong thought a chance to *get* inside your head. Bright thoughts are like sunlight; they can stream into your life and illuminate everything, they can drive the shadows out of your mind and heart. But not if you bolt the door and pull down the shades and refuse to let them in.

It's amazing how many people do just this. They look for the worst in other people instead of the best. They convince themselves—and will try to convince you—that the world is going to Hades in a hand-basket. They take some minor ailment and with the aid of some intensive hypochondria build it up into a major health crisis. If they have money, they worry about losing it. If they don't have it, they worry about that. They act as if the universe is part of a vast plot designed to thwart and frustrate them. It's almost as if they get a gloomy pleasure out of making themselves miserable.

Now, this situation can be corrected. Religion can do it. I have seen it happen time and again. A person surrenders himself to Jesus Christ, asks for help and forgiveness, opens his heart to the vast, healing forces of Christianity—and has his whole life and outlook changed. This is the process known as conversion. It can happen in a dramatic flash, the way lightning can illuminate a dark landscape at night. When it does happen, good thoughts come flooding in and drive out the bad. Joy replaces gloom; hope drives out despair. It's a tremendous and exciting thing to watch, and I have seen it many times.

I think it can happen without religion, too, although it is far more difficult. It is much harder because the person is fighting alone. He has to face up to the fact that he *needs* to be changed—quite a trick in itself. Then he has to set to work changing his attitudes from negative to positive. It's a tough, hard struggle, because his old mental habits will fight him every step of the way. His soul will be encrusted with them, the way the hull of a ship can be encrusted with barnacles. He will have to scrape them off, painfully and laboriously, before he can begin to slip easily and naturally through the waters of life.

To anyone who wants to try this challenging transformation, I can offer one bit of practical advice in five wizard words—wizard because they can work wonders. Those words are: *get your mind off yourself*. Ninety-nine times out of a hundred, when bad thoughts are holding good thoughts out of your mind, it's because they are selfish thoughts, thoughts that revolve only around how *you* are feeling, how *you* are being affected, how *you* are reacting to whatever is happening in your world.

The only way to lick this egocentricity is to hurl yourself into something that makes you forget yourself and enables you to focus on something else. That something else can be a job, it can be church or civic work, it can be a useful or productive hobby, it can simply be a sustained effort to make someone else happy or less unhappy. But once you do it, once you take charge of yourself and make this basic shift in emphasis, the clouds that darken your life will begin to lift.

I can give you a simple and faintly comic example from my own experience. A year or so ago, when I was coming home from Europe on the S.S. *Constitution*, we ran into the edge of a hurricane. Now I must say, bad weather at sea has always been a problem to me. For years I tried all sorts of remedies: Dramamine, baked potatoes, ginger ale, all the things people recommend. But nothing helped until this incident on the S.S. *Constitution*.

The ship was bucking like a demented horse. I was lying on my bed in my cabin, thinking pale green thoughts, when the door opened and in came a cheery fellow who had a cabin down the corridor. I was in no mood for visitors, certainly not cheery ones. He looked at me and said, "What are you doing, lying there in bed?"

"Well," I said, "I'm meditating."

"You could meditate much better up on deck," he said. "Let's go up and look at the storm."

"I don't want to look at it," I said. "Kindly go away."

"Let me read you something," he said. He took out a booklet and read me a passage about the importance of facing up to difficulties, of realizing that you can do anything you want to do if you will just take authority over your weaknesses and fears. "How do you like that?" he wanted to know.

I was not very impressed. "Who wrote it?" I croaked.

"You did," he said. "This is one of your printed sermons."

Well, that shamed me into it. I struggled to my feet and somehow got dressed. We went up on deck and started to walk, and I tell you, I'll never forget that experience as long as I live. Mountainous waves came racing at us like avalanches, the wind ripping the spray off their crests like smoke. Great streamers of spume lashed our faces and soaked our clothes. I could taste the salt on my lips. The deck heaved, the gale shrieked in our ears, but the ship was more than equal to it. She kept slamming into the great seas, butting her way forward, never faltering. I was lost in admiration—admiration of nature's power and fury, and the courage and ingenuity of the puny creature called man who had built this ship and could drive it through the teeth of such a storm.

My friend shouted in my ear: "Isn't this great!" I nodded that it was. My seasickness was completely gone. "Down below," my friend shouted, "you were lying there thinking error; up here you're thinking truth!"

Well, he was a Christian Scientist, and that was one way of putting it. I'd say that down below I had been thinking exclusively about Norman Vincent Peale and how miserable he was. Up on deck I was thinking about the splendor and magnificence of God's angry ocean, and the skill and steadfastness of seafaring men. The shift in emphasis from self to non-self cured my seasickness. It opened a door and let the good thoughts in that drove out the bad.

Five wizard words: *get your mind off yourself*. Try it sometime. You'll see.

CHAPTER X

The Quest for Self-Mastery

And so we come, finally, to the last chapter. It seems—and is—a long time since my solitary walk in the summer moonlight when the idea of writing a book on the moral challenges of our time first occurred to me. But writing it has been an exciting challenge in itself. Something in me will be sorry when it's over.

What can I add now to what I have already said? I have stated and restated my theme: the need for strong inner controls to replace the crumbling outer ones, the need for inner-directedness in an increasingly directionless world, the desperate need in all of us for the kind of responsibility to self and society and the human race that alone can lift man to his full stature in this difficult and demanding world.

Perhaps in my sense of urgency I have harped on this one string too often, but I do not feel apologetic. It was Epictetus, I believe, who said that repetition is the master of studies. It was true when he said it nineteen centuries ago, and it's true today.

Still, in the course of discussing these great challenges, I have offered so many suggestions and exhortations that perhaps, here at the end, I should summarize a bit, try to condense my thoughts into a few small parcels that you can tuck into your pocket and carry away with you.

Let's assume—hopefully—that in the pages of this book I've convinced you of the importance of this quest for self-mastery. Let's assume that you are really sold on the idea, that you want to move up to that higher rung on the moral ladder where you really belong. What are the essential things to keep in mind? What should you *remember* out of all the things we have been talking about here?

I think it all comes down to three things: an attitude, a decision, and an action. Let me explain this as clearly and simply as I can.

185

The attitude, the state of mind that I hope you will take away from this book, is the attitude of *caring*. You have to care about life, about people, about yourself. You have to be truly concerned about your place in the moral state of things. You have to believe that what you do and what you are really matter, and matter deeply. Only then will this quest for self-mastery begin to seem so urgent and important that you know you must undertake it, no matter how difficult it may be.

In talking about importance, I'm not urging anyone to be egotistical or conceited. I'm simply asking you not to under-estimate yourself. My friend Dr. Blanton tells me that in his practice of psychiatry he finds a tendency to self-disparage-ment, a lack of self-esteem, to be the most common problem that he has to deal with. All too often, he says, such peo-ple don't bother to try to control or improve themselves be-cause some gloomy, nagging voice within them keeps whis-pering that they are failures, that they are nobodies, that whether they are good or bad or indifferent makes no real difference, that they can't affect the world in which they live anyway, so why try?

What dreadful, defeatist nonsense! Every word you utter, every deed you do—yes, every thought you think—has an effect somewhere. Each of us is the center of a web of in-terpersonal relationships that never ends. And as communi-cations improve, as distances shrink, the potential impact of one person on many others becomes stronger all the time. As someone has eloquently said, "The world is now too dangerous for anything but truth, too small for anything but brotherhood." It is indeed.

Every day of my life I come across situations where the im-portance of the ordinary, everyday individual is highlighted and dramatized. In Chicago not long ago a young married woman—intelligent, wealthy, popular—found herself worry-ing about the state of the world and wondering what she could do about it. Finally she did something that was—given her rather sophisticated background—quite remarkable. She went to her next-door neighbor and said, "Mary, you can laugh if you like, or say no if you want to, but would you consider meeting with me once a month, just the two of us, to pray for the world?"

Her friend looked at her, startled and serious. Then she said, "Let's make it once a week."

So these women got together, and soon others joined them, and before long they had quite a prayer group functioning. Then one day, after prayers for the world, one girl said, "I wonder if I might bring up something personal?" She went on to discuss certain marital difficulties she had been having. Other women brought up similar problems, and the group tried to help them find solutions.

It soon became evident to these young women that they could not hope to reform the world unless they began with themselves and their immediate environment. They invited their husbands to join the group, and help combat the widespread subterranean immorality that was the cause of so many of their personal problems. The results were so far-reaching that eventually the whole community was changed. So, you see, the initial effort of one hesitant, groping individual in the end revolutionized dozens of lives. Important? You never know just how important you may be!

So much for the attitude I hope you'll carry away with you. What about the decision?

The decision is this: You must make up your mind to shift your control center from outside to inside. This is not just any decision; it is the all-important decision, because once you've made it, it tends to release the power you will need to carry it out!

How does this decision release power in you? It does it by eliminating the fears and resentments and blocks and frustrations that are always associated with rules or restrictions when they are imposed from without.

Psychiatrists say that all of us carry over some of this resentment from childhood, when we had to accept parental regulations and commands and corrections all the time. They add that if we keep on living solely by external rules, always being controlled by fear of punishment or fear of authority, some of this anger keeps smoldering in us, blocking growth and expansion, dampening creativity.

So what we have to do is realign our attitudes where all this is concerned. We have to admit to ourselves that to a large extent, in the past, our lives have been governed and directed by fear. And the astonishing thing is that once we do, this very admission and realization act as a great release mechanism, a method of clearing away the resentments and blocks that have prevented us from acting as responsible, self-controlled individuals. We are suddenly free, the chains drop away, an extraordinary surge of power and confidence comes to us. And we are then able to act as we should act, not because we're afraid not to, but because we want to!

This decision to be ruled by yourself can make a difference in even the smallest aspects of your everyday life. You're driving along a highway, let's say, and you see a sign informing you that the speed limit is dropping from sixty miles per hour to forty for the next few miles. Now if you regard that sign *only* as a symbol of authority, if you obey it *only* because you are afraid of being arrested, a little flash of anger will explode in you, a little vibration of resentment will be set up that can subtly affect your whole outlook. You may be so exasperated, in fact, that you drive faster, just to show your distaste for external authority of any kind.

But if you are an inner-directed person, you don't react this way. You accept the sign as valuable information, which it is. You assume that it is the reasonable and intelligent speed for that particular stretch of road. Far from resenting the people who put it there, you actually feel a sense of gratitude. And what has happened? Your shift in attitude has transformed you from an unconsciously angry driver (which automatically makes you highly dangerous on the road) to a relaxed and cheerful one!

What I am trying to say is that there is all the difference in the world between being controlled by fear and being controlled by your own free choice. The former limits, confines, deadens. The latter liberates, frees, strengthens. This means that somewhere, somehow, each of us must find the determination and the intelligence to shift from a kind of sullen and resentful submission to external controls to a cheerful acceptance of inner controls, that no longer seem restrictive because we *choose* to live by them.

Try making this key decision in your own life. Try to right now, as you sit reading these lines. Then watch, as the days go by, to see if it doesn't begin to release a hidden power within you. I'm confident that it will.

Now, making that decision is essential, but there is still one more thing that you must do. You may see the importance of changing certain things in your life, you may make up your mind to change, but nothing significant is going to happen until you *act*, until you begin by doing one specific thing that proves that you are a different person with a different approach to things.

There is a verse in the Bible that hammers home the importance of this. In the Gospel according to St. John, Jesus says, "If ye know these things, happy are ye *if ye do them.*" The implication is crystal clear: It's not enough just to have wisdom in your head; you must put it into action in your life. Mere knowledge of the importance of inner control isn't sufficient; *you must demonstrate it.*

This sequence is inescapable. Every great endeavor begins with a thought, but the thought must be followed by a visible act. I was thinking about this the other night when I was reading a biography of William Lloyd Garrison, whose life was one long struggle against the vile institution of slavery. Few people stop to think any longer of how deeply entrenched that evil was in American life just a little over a century ago. In those days many people actually believed that without slavery civilization could not progress. That's what the Governor of South Carolina said in 1835. As late as 1855, the Moderator of the Presbyterian Church said that "God has permitted slavery for wise reasons."

So slavery was rooted in custom, in business, in politics, even in religion. But Garrison thought it was wrong. He must have hesitated, he must have been filled with doubts. But the time came when he acted, he spoke out. And this initial act of protest unleashed a torrent of energy in him. "With what a lash," wrote his biographer, "he must have cracked his thoughts against the thin skins of our ancestors!" Do you remember what he said? His words have come ringing down the years. He said, "I will be as harsh as truth and as uncompromising as justice." When people tried to silence him, he cried: "I will not equivocate; I will not excuse; I will not retreat a single inch; and I will be heard!" Thirty-two years after Garrison began his lonely struggle, Abraham Lincoln dealt slavery its death blow with his Emancipation Proclamation. But the great fight was led by Garrison, and his fight must have begun with a single act . . . not a theory, not a hypothesis, not a silent, inward conclusion, but an act.

So before this day is out, do something specific and concrete that will demonstrate your determination to change yourself and your life for the better. Pay a debt. Heal a broken relationship. End a quarrel. Offer an apology. Pray for someone—out loud. Visit someone who is sick, or a shut-in. Restrain yourself from buying something you had planned to buy for yourself and give the money to charity instead.

Do whatever you do quietly, without ostentation. And do it, not from fear of punishment or hope of reward, but simply because you want to do it, because you prefer to be an inner-directed person.

Only when an act of will is accompanied or followed quickly by visible action does the whole process become a part of the person and lead to further action, further commitment. This is why, in religious conversion, ministers used to issue the invitation to converts to "come forward to the altar rail." They knew that this physical act of affirmation, this public demonstration was often necessary to confirm and establish the inner change of heart and personality. Billy Graham uses this technique constantly in his crusades. And I have used it myself, even in a staid Fifth Avenue church, with impressive results.

Don't content yourself with passive acceptance; break the inertia of the past with a positive, dynamic act, and you will find that you have released hidden powers that will make subsequent acts seem easy by comparison.

So there you have the three things that I hope you'll remember long after you have closed this book: the importance of yourself as a moral force in this world, the shift from outer to inner controls, and the final necessity of making a move.

Are these steps so difficult? I don't think so. I believe they are well within the capability of any one of us. I also believe that if enough people would take them today, we might wake up in a different and better world tomorrow.

I'll go beyond that. I'll go so far as to say that I believe this world-change is coming anyway. The moral chaos around us is dark and menacing, it's true. But as the saying goes, not all the darkness in the world can put out the light of one small candle. Even as I write, many candles are being lighted by aroused, dedicated, inner-directed people. Mark my words, a moral counter-revolution is coming. We may well be standing on the threshold of a new era of moral greatness. And it will be ushered in by people who have learned how to master and control and govern themselves.

Pessimists may disagree. I can almost hear their skeptical voices. "Oh," they may say, "you're hopelessly optimistic. It has taken man a million years to reach even this dubious stage of development. What makes you think he can make this great leap forward in the next few years or decades? What makes you think the masses can learn to control and discipline themselves, even if a few enlightened individuals do?"

My reply to this would be that the "masses" are made up of people, and I believe in people. I think almost any person can be educated to do almost anything. Furthermore, the means of vastly accelerated forms of education are already in our hands: radio, television, sensationally improved teaching techniques. Today people can communicate with one another on a scale undreamed of fifty years ago; knowledge can pass from person to person with tremendous speed. This, after all, is the great gift that separates man from the animals. Only man can accumulate knowledge and wisdom, and pass them on.

And I am not alone in my optimism. The great souls of history have always had this faith in man's capacity for growth and self-improvement. Hiding in her attic from the Nazi terror that finally took her life, the young Jewish girl Anne Frank could still write in her diary: "In spite of everything, I still believe that people are good at heart." What faith, and what courage!

Indeed, where man's capacity for expansion and enlightenment is concerned, I have the best of all authorities on my side—Christ Himself. Who had more faith in people than He? Publicans, tax-extortionists, prostitutes, sinners of all kinds—He saw the potential for self-correction in all of them, as He saw it in everyone. He put no limitation on the power of the human spirit to lift itself above itself. He told His friends that they were the salt of the earth, the light of the world, that He loved them for what they were and what they could become. He believed in the greatness of people, real or potential. And if He did, why shouldn't I?

It *can* be achieved, this inner-directedness that I have been writing about all this time, it *can* be acquired, it *can* be won. Not easily, perhaps, not instantly, not without trial and error and setbacks and failures. But even the attempt is worthwhile, because every step toward the distant goal brings its own satisfactions and its own rewards.

Perhaps the final goal of complete self-mastery can never be reached in this life, but some people come very close. I have always remembered a story about Renoir, the great French painter, that I read long ago. For years, Renoir suffered dreadfully with arthritis. His hands were twisted and deformed; the joints of his fingers were swollen and enor-

mous. At last he reached a point where he could only hold
the brush clumsily with thumb and forefinger, high up in the
cleft between them, because there was no power in the finger. Still he worked on. His condition became so bad that he
had to be carried to his easel. Attendants had to move the
canvas for him, because he could only paint directly in front
of his hand. But he never complained. He remained cheerful and serene. And he kept on working.

One day Matisse came to call and found Renoir painting
as usual. At one point he winced with pain, and the brush fell
from his hand. Torn with pity, Matisse cried, "Why torture
yourself like this, Master? You have done so much. You may
well be satisfied!"

Renoir looked at him and smiled. "The pain passes, Matisse," he said, "but the beauty remains."

Not many of us, perhaps, could face adversity with such
nobility. But there is something in all of us that responds to
challenge. In the final analysis, it is not to the siren call of
safety and security and self-indulgence that the souls of men
respond. It is to sacrifice and hardship and danger.

All great leaders have known this. What did Garibaldi
promise his little band of followers. Wealth? Fame? Fortune?
He said, "I offer you neither pay, nor quarters, nor provisions.
I offer hunger, forced marches, battles, death." What did
Winston Churchill promise his beleaguered countrymen?
Blood and toil, sweat and tears. "Blessed are ye," said Jesus,
"when men shall revile you, and persecute you, and shall
say all manner of evil against you falsely, for my sake."

These great leaders offered no tangible, no material rewards
at all. But when they called for sacrifice, they got it on a
scale past all reckoning.

Surely this spark in the human spirit is not dead. Surely
it will still respond to a call for self-discipline and self-
control, for a return to honor and to rightness. Let us, then,
demand these things of ourselves. Let us face up to the
choice that God is offering our generation. Let us move forward, out of the moral confusion and darkness that surround
us, to a new era of enlightenment in which inner-directed
men choose goodness because they are free to choose—
and in so doing move ever closer to the kingdom of God.